# CHUNKY
# KNITS

# CHUNKY KNITS

### COZY HATS, SCARVES AND MORE
### MADE SIMPLE WITH EXTRA-LARGE YARN

**ALYSSARHAYE GRACIANO**

FOUNDER OF BLACKSHEEPMADE

PAGE STREET
PUBLISHING CO.

PAGE STREET
PUBLISHING CO.

First published in 2020 by Alyssarhaye Graciano

Page Street Publishing Co.

27 Congress Street, Suite 105

Salem, MA  01970

www.pagestreetpublishing.com

Distributed by Macmillan, sales in Canada by The Canadian Manda Group.

24    23    22    21    20      1   2   3   4   5

ISBN-13: 978-1-62414-956-6

ISBN-10:  1-62414-956-1

Library of Congress Control Number:  2019951531

Cover and book design by Laura Benton for Page Street Publishing Co.

Photography by Kenneth Hamlett

Photo on page 26 by Alyssarhaye Graciano

Printed and bound in the United States

Page Street Publishing protects our planet by donating to nonprofits like The Trustees, which focuses on local land conservation.

TO EVERYTHING I IGNORED
BECAUSE OF THIS BOOK,

TO MY PARENTS,
FOR THEIR ENCOURAGEMENT,

AND TO CHRIS,
FOR CLEANING THE HOUSE
WHILE I KNIT FOR THE
LAST YEAR(S).

# CONTENTS

INTRODUCTION 9

## SCARVES

**STATEMENT WRAPS AND EVERYDAY WEARS FOR BLIZZARDS AND BREEZES** 12

TILIKUM SCARF 15

BOBO SCARF 19

ROSE CITY SCARF 20

WILLAMETTE SCARF 24

LOMBARD SCARF 28

HELLA BIG ARM KNIT SCARF 32

LENNY SCARF 36

NANAY'S SCARF 39

## COWLS

**QUICK INFINITY-STYLE SCARVES FOR MOVERS, SHAKERS AND DO-ERS** 40

RHAYE COWL 43

CASCADES COWL 44

LA TORTUGA COWL 47

CLARK COWL 48

MORRISON COWL 51

CHELSEA ARM KNIT COWL 52

RADIUS HOODED COWL 55

## BEANIES

**FROM SKULLCAPS TO EARFLAPS, HATS FOR THE WHOLE FAMILY** 58

MULTNOMAH BEANIE 61

PNW BEANIE 65

CADA DÍA BEANIE 69

MISS VAN'S BALACLAVA 70

DON'S NIGHT CAP 74

## FURRY FRIENDS

**OUR PETS NEED SOME HANDMADE LOVE, TOO** 76

TUG-O-WAR TOY 79

JAX SCARF 80

WINSTON'S MAT 83

PACO 'S PILLOW 84

# HOME

**MODERN KNITS FOR**
**COZYING UP INDOORS**            **86**

EMBER'S CIRCLE RUG                89

RHYTHM RUG                        90

BLACKSHEEP'S ARM KNIT
BLANKET                           93

HOMEBODY BLANKET                  94

YAMHILL BLANKET                   98

WALTER'S OTTOMAN                  101


STITCH ABBREVIATIONS             105

TECHNIQUES                        109

YARN                              127

ACKNOWLEDGMENTS                   131

ABOUT THE AUTHOR                  133

INDEX                             135

# INTRODUCTION

This is going to sound like I'm being extra, but chunky yarns saved my life (and time)! When I first tried knitting in sixth grade, I chose the fluffiest yarn possible. It was soft, fuzzy and not too thin, but I couldn't see where the actual stitches were, and I kept splitting the fibers. Safe to say I gave up just a couple of inches into my scarf.

I tried again when I was a senior in high school. I had picked up crochet and thought I would give knitting another go. This time I chose the plainest, least fuzzy yarn, but it was way too thin! Projects took more time than I was willing to spend. I solved that problem by doubling the yarn but didn't like the end result. I knit a few hats and put knitting back down for another two years.

In 2014, I received a scholarship to study abroad in Costa Rica where I would help save endangered sea turtles. What in the world does this have to do with knitting?! Well, let me tell ya! I needed to fund my trip and I needed to do it fast. I thought, "I can knit beanies . . . And if I use chunky yarn, I'll be done in no time!"

Fast-forward to three months later: I was using every chunky yarn I could find. Knitting up beanies, scarves, cowls; never following any patterns. I just knit what I liked. Turns out other folks liked it too because I was able to fund my entire trip, flight included! Thus, BlackSheepMade was born. I realized I could make a career out of my passion for knitting.

BlackSheepMade creates handmade fiber goods for you, your home and your pets! I hand make everything myself by way of knitting, crochet, macramé and weaving. While it started out as a hobby, knitting individual custom pieces and consignment for local shops, I now teach workshops across the West Coast, create art installations and design patterns for myself and other brands. BlackSheepMade has brought me many incredible opportunities, such as this book!

Now, five years later, I have compiled all of my tips and tricks into one book for you all to use! Whether you want to start your own knitting business or simply want to learn a new hobby, *Chunky Knits* will guide you through the world of chunky yarn and all of its accessories. In *Chunky Knits*, you'll learn how to knit large color-block scarves, different ways to seam up a cowl, how to knit in the round if seaming just isn't your jam and a few other tricks I've learned along the way. These tips and tricks will lead you to wearable, everyday knits that will look good on you and your favorite furry friend, as well as in your home!

By using bulkier yarns, these projects can be done in as little as two hours or just a single weekend. The bulky weight allows you to knit up what could be more time-consuming projects in a fraction of the time. I am what I would call a procrasti-knitter. I often wait until the last minute to knit up orders. Thicker, bulkier yarn allows me to do so because it works up so quickly.

One of the things I love most about chunky yarn is that you're able to see your stitches. No more guessing if you're inserting your needle in the right loop or accidentally adding stitches. The stitches are so large that when you mess up, you'll be able to trace your steps and fix your mistakes without a major freak out. Chunky yarn is very forgiving. You'll be able to see where your needles are going during complicated stitches, make grand motifs simply because the yarn is already big, and most importantly, stay warm!

With this added ease, a knitter can feel more confident when trying out a new stitch. The patterns in this book are split up in three different levels of difficulty: Casual Knitter, Adventurous Knitter and Granny-Level Knitter. If you're a beginner with a few basic stitches in your toolbox (knit, purl, k2tog) start with the Casual Knitter patterns. If you've dabbled with more involved stitches like Herringbone or have tried colorwork, the Adventurous Knitter patterns are for you. Granny-Level Knitters should be able to handle complex stitches, colorwork and shaping simultaneously.

Before starting a pattern in this book, I recommend taking a look at the abbreviations and techniques that will be used for that specific pattern. Check out the Stitch Abbreviations appendix (page 105) and Techniques guide (page 109).

Now let's talk supplies. Big yarn requires big needles. I like to use circular needles for the majority of my projects. These needles tend to be shorter than straight needles and therefore less cumbersome. If you've knit with thinner, lighter weight yarns, you'll know it's pretty easy to fit your WIP (work in progress) in a small project bag and take it around town. With chunkier yarn, your projects grow quite quickly and make travel-knitting a bit inconvenient. Don't get me wrong—you can definitely find me at a coffee shop takin' up two tables and a chair with my chunky WIP! But if your yarn is already bulky, it helps if your needles are a bit shorter and more manageable. Circular needles also have a cord in between—all the extra room for thick stitches without being in the way! They ease travel knitting and allow you to pause in the middle of projects.

For a couple of projects in this book, your needles will be your arms. Yep, you read that right. In *Chunky Knits*, you'll learn how to arm knit, a fiber phenomenon. We'll dive into more detail about arm knitting when we get to those patterns, but be ready for a good upper body workout! Feel free to skip arm day at the gym.

If you plan to substitute yarn for any of these patterns, head to my yarn resource page (page 127). Not only do I list my favorite tools but also chunky yarns I have grown to love throughout my knitting journey.

My big hope for this book is that you learn something new. Whether that means a new stitch pattern, a new construction technique or a yarn you aren't familiar with, my goal here is to teach you and share the joy knitting has brought me!

*Chunky Knits* helped me quit my day job and pursue my creative dreams full-time, becoming the Granny-Level Knitter I have always wanted to be. I hope these patterns help you advance in your knitting journey, and I am so excited to see what you've learned from my book!

Now let's get knitting!

*AlyssaRhaye Graciano*

# SCARVES

STATEMENT WRAPS AND EVERYDAY WEARS FOR BLIZZARDS AND BREEZES

**SCARVES ARE BASICALLY BLANKETS** that are acceptable to wear in public, especially when using chunkier yarns! In this section, you will find long, open-ended scarves that can be worn a multitude of ways. Wrap 'em once, twice, tuck 'em or even lay in them.

The first four scarves in this section will highlight the intarsia technique (page 119), which allows for big blocks of colorwork and makes switching colors simple. Add a chunky yarn to that and you'll learn intarsia in seconds! A bulky yarn will highlight exactly which yarn you're knitting with and when to switch. Once you learn my patterns, feel free to experiment with your own designs! Where would you place big patches of color? In what shape? The possibilities are endless.

Other scarves in this chapter are simply giant and gorgeous. You'll learn how to knit the Hella Big Arm Knit Scarf (page 32), inspired by Lenny Kravitz's iconic blanket scarf, a ridiculously large scarf that should technically be for giants or New York Fashion Week.

Although all of these scarves are quite generous in length, the weight of the yarn helps your project work up rather quickly, giving you an immediate sense of accomplishment and satisfaction. This alone has helped me complete chunky projects time after time, unlike all of my worsted weight WIPs that have remained WIPs for the last three years. If you struggle with marathon-length knitting projects, then perhaps chunky projects are for you. They will take up much less time and you'll be showing off your creations after a weekend of knitting as opposed to next year.

# TILIKUM SCARF

The Tilikum Scarf is named after Tilikum Crossing Bridge, which is located on Chinook land in Portland, Oregon. It depicts the bridge's cable-stayed engineering. Cables support the weight of the bridge as they run down from towers to the deck of the bridge, creating a triangle pattern. This triangle pattern is created in the scarf by way of intarsia, a colorwork technique that avoids having to weave in multiple ends. If you're new to intarsia, head to page 119 for step-by-step instructions.

While the Tilikum Scarf final measurements are 9 x 80 inches (22 x 200 cm), with chunky yarns it can knit up in a few hours! I enjoy making this scarf for that reason alone. It makes for a quick gift but features a modern design that will give the impression that you're a pro knitter (because you are!). Out of all my scarves that feature intarsia in this chapter, the Tilikum is my favorite because it is the simplest but has a big effect.

## YARN

Wool and the Gang Crazy Sexy Wool (7 ounces [200 g], 87 yards [80 m] 100% wool):

- 2 balls Eagle Grey (Color A). 174 yards (159 m) used
- 1 ball Cinnamon Dust (Color B).
- 1 ball Bronzed Olive (Color C).

## GAUGE

In garter st, 6 sts and 12 rows = 4 inches (10 cm). To save time, take time to check gauge.

## FINISHED MEASUREMENTS

9 x 80 inches (23 x 200 cm)

## NEEDLES

US 19 (15-mm) straight or 24- or 36-inch (61- or 91-cm) circular needles, or size needed to obtain correct gauge

## NOTIONS

Darning needle or crochet hook for weaving in ends

## TECHNIQUES

Intarsia (page 119)

Garter Stitch (page 115)

## DESIGNER NOTE

For the even rows in this pattern, match the color to the previous row. For example, if the previous row said k9 in Color A and k6 in Color B, the following row would be k6 in Color B and then k9 in Color A. This also applies to the Bobo Scarf (page 19), Rose City Scarf (page 20) and Willamette Scarf (page 24).

## NOW LET'S GET KNITTING!

CO 15 sts.

## SOLID SECTION 1

ROWS 1–6: Using Color A, K across.

## FIRST TRIANGLE

ROW 1: K12 in Color A. Join Color B by tying a loose knot and leave a 4-inch (10-cm) tail to weave in later. K the last 3 sts using Color B.

ROW 2 (and all even rows): K across, using the same color for each st as the previous row and using the intarsia technique when changing colors.

ROW 3: K11 in Color A, switch colors, k4 in Color B.

ROW 5: K10 in Color A, switch, k5 in Color B.

CONTINUE in this manner, knitting 1 fewer st in Color A, switching, and knitting 1 more st in Color B on odd-numbered rows until you have knit 4 sts in Color A and 11 sts in Color B (Row 17).

ROW 19: K3 in Color A, switch, k12 in Color B.

(CONTINUED)

ROW 2 (and all even rows): K across, using the same color for each st as the previous row and using the intarsia technique when changing colors.

ROW 3: K4 in Color B, switch colors, k11 in Color A.

ROW 5: K5 in Color B, switch, k10 in Color A.

CONTINUE in this manner, knitting 1 more st in Color B, switching, and knitting 1 fewer st in Color A on odd-numbered rows until you have knit 11 sts in Color B and 4 sts in Color A (Row 17).

ROW 19: K12 in Color B, switch, k3 in Color A.

ROW 21: Attach Color C and k12. Switch colors and k3 in Color A. Cut Color B, leaving a long enough tail to weave in later.

ROW 23: K11 in Color C, switch, k4 in Color A.

ROW 25: K10 in Color C, switch, k5 in Color A.

CONTINUE in this manner, knitting 1 fewer st in Color C, and 1 more st in Color A on odd-numbered rows until you have knit 4 sts in Color C and 11 sts in Color A (Row 37).

ROW 39: K3 in Color C, switch, k12 in Color A.

ROW 40: K across, using the same color for each st as the previous row and using the intarsia technique when changing colors.

## SOLID SECTION 3
CUT Color C, leaving a tail long enough to weave in later. Using Color A, k 42 inches (107 cm) in garter st (126 rows/63 garter ridges) or to desired scarf length less 16 inches (41 cm).

## THIRD TRIANGLE
REPEAT first triangle.

## SOLID SECTION 4
CUT Color C. K 8 rows in Color A.

## FINISHING
BO loosely.

WEAVE IN the ends and your Tilikum Scarf is ready to wear!

ROW 21: K3 in Color A, attach Color C, k12 in Color C. Cut Color B, leaving a long enough tail to weave in later.

ROW 23: K4 in Color A, switch, k11 in Color C.

ROW 25: K5 in Color A, switch, k10 in Color C.

CONTINUE in this manner, knitting 1 more st in Color A, and 1 fewer st in Color C on odd-numbered rows until you have knit 11 sts in Color A and 4 sts in Color C (Row 37).

ROW 39: K12 in Color A, switch, k3 in Color C.

ROW 40: K across, using the same color for each st as the previous row and using the intarsia technique when changing colors.

## SOLID SECTION 2
CUT Color C. K 8 rows using Color A. Cut Color A, leaving a tail long enough to weave in later.

## SECOND TRIANGLE
ROW 1: K3 in Color B. Join Color A by tying a loose knot, leaving a 4-inch (10-cm) tail to weave in later. K12 in Color A.

# BOBO SCARF

The Bobo Scarf was made with sustainability in mind, utilizing almost every yard in two skeins of yarn. Its minimalist design highlights the classic garter stitch and intarsia colorwork. It is knit lengthwise and therefore requires longer circular knitting needles.

The scarf's symmetrical design offers versatility to be worn in three different styles, making this an easy staple in your winter wardrobe. Hang it around your neck to showcase the design, wrap it once to make it shorter or wrap it a few times to create a cowl. This pattern is for the sustainable knitter, conscious of their efforts to limit waste on our planet and embracing the slow-fashion lifestyle.

## YARN
Wool and the Gang Crazy Sexy Wool (7 ounces [200 g], 87 yards [80 m], 100% wool):

- 1 ball Eucalyptus Green (Color A)
- 1 ball Dusty Denim (Color B)

## GAUGE
In garter st, 6 sts and 12 rows = 4 inches (10 cm). To save time, take time to check gauge.

## FINISHED MEASUREMENTS
6 x 75 inches (15 x 191 cm)

## NEEDLES
US 19 (15-mm) 40-inch (102-cm) circular needle, or size needed to obtain correct gauge

## NOTIONS
Darning needle or crochet hook for weaving in ends

## TECHNIQUES
Intarsia (page 119)

Garter Stitch (page 115)

## DESIGNER NOTE
For the even rows in this pattern, match the color to the previous row. For example, if the previous row said k9 in Color A and k6 in Color B, the following row would be k6 in Color B and then k9 in Color A. This also applies to the Tilikum Scarf (page 15), Rose City Scarf (page 20) and Willamette Scarf (page 24).

## NOW LET'S GET KNITTING!
CO 112 sts using your preferred method.

ROWS 1–4: Using Color A, k across.

ROW 5: K9 in Color A, join Color B by tying a loose knot, leaving a 4-inch (10-cm) tail to weave in later. K20 in Color B. Continue working in Color A, pulling from the opposite end of your ball, and k to the end of the row.

ROW 6: K across, using the same color for each st as the previous row and using the the intarsia technique when changing colors.

CUT color B, leaving enough of a tail to weave in later.

ROWS 7–8: Using Color A, k 2 rows.

CUT Color A, leaving enough of a tail to weave in later.

ROWS 9–10: Using Color B, k 2 rows.

ROW 11: K in Color B until you reach the last 29 sts, join Color A, k20, k9 using Color B, pulling from the opposite end of your ball.

ROW 12: K across, using the same color for each st as the previous row and using the the intarsia technique when changing colors.

ROW 13–16: K in garter st using Color B.

## FINISHING
BO and weave in all ends.

# ROSE CITY SCARF

The Rose City Scarf features multiple color changes using intarsia and can be the perfect project to really test your new skills! While this pattern may feel daunting due to the many color changes, the bulky yarn allows those changes to be clear and mostly painless.

Named after my current hometown, the Rose City Scarf features large squares patched together with different colors. The blocks remind me of Portland's different areas. Every corner may have its own look and vibe, but you always know you're still in Portland.

## YARN

Wool and the Gang Crazy Sexy Wool
(7 ounces [200 g], 87 yards [80 m] 100% wool),
5 balls total:

- 2 balls (174 yards [159 m]) Rocky Grey (Color A)
- ½ ball (42 yards [38 m]) Duck Egg Blue (Color B)
- ½ ball (42 yards [38 m]) Cinnamon Dust (Color C)
- ½ ball (42 yards [38 m]) Bronzed Olive (Color D)

## GAUGE

In garter st, 6 sts and 12 rows = 4 inches (10 cm). To save time, take time to check gauge.

## FINISHED MEASUREMENTS

9 x 70 inches (23 x 178 cm)

## NEEDLES

US 19 (15-mm) straight or 24- or 36-inch (61- or 91-cm) circular needles

## NOTIONS

Darning needle or crochet hook for weaving in ends

## TECHNIQUES

Intarsia (page 119)

Garter Stitch (page 115)

## DESIGNER NOTE

For the even rows in this pattern, match the color to the previous row. For example, if the previous row said k9 in Color A and k6 in Color B, the following row would be k6 in Color B and then k9 in Color A. This also applies to the Tilikum Scarf (page 15), Bobo Scarf (page 19) and Willamette Scarf (page 24).

## NOW LET'S GET KNITTING!

USING COLOR A, CO 15 stitches.

ROWS 1-6: K.

ROW 7: K3 in Color A. Join Color B and k to the end of the row.

ROW 8 (AND ALL EVEN ROWS): K across, using the same color for each st as the previous row and using the intarsia technique when changing colors.

ROWS 9-12: Rep rows 7 and 8 twice more.

ROW 13: K3 in Color A. K4 in color B. Join Color C and k to the end of the row.

ROWS 15-18: Rep rows 13 and 14 twice more.

ROW 19: K3 in Color A. K4 in Color B. K4 in Color C. Join Color D and k to the end of the row.

ROWS 21-26: Rep rows 19 and 20 three more times.

ROWS 27-44: Cut Colors B, C and D, leaving long enough tails to weave in later. K in garter st using Color A.

ROWS 45: Attach Color D and k12. Cut Color A from the beginning of the row and join here. K the remaining 3 sts in Color A.

(CONTINUED)

ROWS 47–50: Rep rows 45 and 46 twice more.

ROW 51: Attach Color B and k8. Cut Color D and reattach here. K4 in Color D then k3 in Color A, using the intarsia technique to switch colors.

ROWS 53–56: Rep rows 51 and 52 twice. Note that you no longer have to cut and reattach colors as they are all now in the correct positions.

ROW 57: Attach Color C and k4. Cut Color B and reattach here. K4 in Color B, k4 in Color D then k3 in Color A, using the intarsia technique to switch colors.

ROWS 59–64: Rep rows 57 and 58 three more times. Note that you no longer have to cut and reattach colors as they are all now in the correct positions.

ROWS 65–144: K in garter st using Color A.

ROW 145: K3 in Color A. Join Color C and k to the end of the row.

ROWS 147–150: Rep rows 145 and 146 twice more.

ROW 151: K3 in Color A. K4 in Color C. Join Color D and k to the end of the row.

ROWS 153–156: Rep rows 151 and 152 twice more.

ROW 157: K3 in Color A. K4 in Color C. K4 in Color D. Join color B and k to the end of the row.

ROWS 159–164: Rep rows 157 and 158 three more times.

ROWS 165–190: Trim Colors B, C and D, leaving long enough tails to weave in later. K in garter stitch using Color A.

## FINISHING
BO and weave in ends.

# WILLAMETTE SCARF

Now, this is not your everyday scarf. Garter stitch, sure that's easy. Intarsia? If you've been knitting in order, you have that down. But what makes it extra special? The loop stitch! The loop stitch adds some extra texture to this wooly beast of a scarf.

I suggest using contrasting colors to really make this scarf pop. A bold palette mixed with its funky texture will be sure to stop some folks on the street! This scarf isn't for the shy!

## YARN
Wool and the Gang Crazy Sexy Wool
(7 ounces [200 g], 87 yards [80 m] 100% wool):

- 2 balls Duck Egg Blue (Color A)
- 2 balls Red Ochre (Color B)

## GAUGE
In garter st, 6 sts and 12 rows = 4 inches (10 cm). This pattern is not overly dependent on gauge.

## FINISHED MEASUREMENTS
10 x 81 inches (25 x 206 cm)

## NEEDLES
US 19 (15-mm) straight or circular needles, or size needed to obtain correct gauge

## NOTIONS
Darning needle or crochet hook for weaving in ends

## TECHNIQUES
Garter Stitch (page 115)

Intarsia (page 119)

Loop Stitch (page 121)

## DESIGNER NOTE
For the even rows in this pattern, match the color to the previous row. For example, if the previous row said k9 in Color A and k6 in Color B, the following row would be k6 in Color B and then k9 in Color A. This also applies to the Tilikum Scarf (page 15), Bobo Scarf (page 19) and Rose City Scarf (page 20).

## NOW LET'S GET KNITTING!
USING COLOR A, CO 12 sts.

ROWS 1-6: K across using Color A.

## STAIR STEP SECTION 1
ROW 7: Join Color B by tying a loose knot, leaving a 4-inch (10-cm) tail to weave in later. K3 with Color B, k9 with Color A.

ROWS 8-12: K across, using the same color for each st as the previous row and using the intarsia technique when changing colors.

ROW 13: Using Color B, k6, k6 with Color A.

ROWS 14-18: K across, using the same colors as before.

ROW 19: Using Color B, k9, k3 with Color A.

ROWS 20-24: K across, using the same colors as before.

CUT Color A.

ROWS 25-30: K across using Color B.

(CONTINUED)

## STAIR STEP SECTION 2

ROW 31: Attach Color A. With Color A, k3 loop sts, k9 with Color B.

ROWS 32-36: K across, using the same color for each st as the previous row and using the the intarsia technique when changing colors. Note that the loop stitches are only for Row 31. Knit regular knit stitches for rows 32-36.

ROW 37: Using Color A, k3, k3 loop sts, with Color B, k6.

ROWS 38-42: K across, using the same color for each st as the previous row and using the the intarsia technique when changing colors.

ROW 43: Using Color A, k6, k3 loop sts, with Color B, k3.

ROWS 44-48: K across, using the same colors as before.

CUT Color B.

ROWS 49: Using Color A, k9, k3 loop sts.

ROWS 50-54: K across using Color A.

ROWS 55-198: Rep Stair Step Sections 1 and 2 three more times. (You will have four sections with loops.)

ROWS 199-222: Rep Stair Step Section 1 one more time.

## FINISHING

BO and weave in all ends.

# LOMBARD SCARF

Although the majority of this scarf is knit in garter stitch, it involves a mini cable (T2B), creating raised stitches that travel across your scarf. The raised slants pop against the garter stitch background creating a minimalist's dream. Solid color, slight texture . . . Perfection! This scarf is great practice for anyone who wants to get into cable work but is daunted by the classic cable where multiple stitches are being moved around. Here, you only need to worry about two stitches at a time!

## YARN
Wool and the Gang Crazy Sexy Wool
(7 ounces [200 g], 87 yards [80 m] 100% wool):

- 3 balls Primary Grey

## GAUGE
In garter st, 6 sts and 12 rows = 4 inches (10 cm).
To save time, take time to check gauge.

## FINISHED MEASUREMENTS
9½ x 85 inches (24 x 216 cm)

## NEEDLES
US 19 (15-mm) straight or circular needles, or size needed to obtain correct gauge

## NOTIONS
4 stitch markers

Darning needle or crochet hook for weaving in ends

## TECHNIQUE
Garter Stitch (page 115)

## DESIGNER NOTE
This pattern uses markers that are placed and removed on every RS row within the T2B (twist two back [page 106]). Keeping these markers showing up in the right places is key to getting these twisted stitches to travel.

## NOW LET'S GET KNITTING!
CO 15 sts.

ROWS 1–2: K.

## TRACK 1 OF TRAVELLING ST
ROW 3: K until you have 3 sts left. T2B, k last stitch.

ROW 4 (WS): K up to marker, sm, p1, k to end of row.

ROW 5 (RS): K until 2 sts before marker, T2B, remove old marker, k to end of row.

ROWS 6–13: Rep Rows 4 and 5 four times.

ROW 14: K up to marker, sm, p1, k to end of row.

## TRACK 2 OF TRAVELLING ST
ROW 15: K until 2 sts before marker, T2B, rm, k2, T2B, k3.

ROW 16 (WS): *K up to marker, sm, p1; rep from *, k to end of row.

ROW 17 (RS): *K until 2 sts before marker. T2B, rm; rep from *, k to end of row.

ROWS 18–25: Rep Rows 16 and 17 four times.

ROW 26: *K up to marker, sm, p1; rep from *, k to end of row.

(CONTINUED)

## FINISH UP TRACK 2

ROW 27: K up to marker, rm, k until 2 sts before marker, T2B, rm, k to end of row.

ROW 28 (WS): K up to marker, sm, p1, k to end of row.

ROW 29 (RS): K until 2 sts before marker, T2B, rm, k to end of row.

ROWS 30-35: Rep Rows 28 and 29 three times.

ROW 36: K up to marker, sm, p1, k to end of row.

REPEAT Rows 3-36 six more times.

ROWS 241 AND 242: K across.

## FINISHING

BO and weave in all ends.

# HELLA BIG ARM KNIT SCARF

Get those arms ready, because it's time to arm knit! This pattern features the ever-popular technique of arm knitting, using your arms as the needles. The novel idea of using your arms as giant knitting needles blew up across the internet, leaving us all wanting to try it out ourselves. If you don't feel like using your arms, you can use US 50 (25-mm) knitting needles.

I knit how my abuelita cooks. I never really measure anything; always just a bit of making it up as I go. I set out to make a blanket, casting on enough stitches to cover one person's body. But then I got carried away in the motion of arm knitting, almost like a runner's high and kept going and going and going . . . Eventually it turned into a seven-foot (2-m)-long blanket and as a joke, I took a photo of myself wearing it like a scarf. Folks actually asked for their own! So here we are: The Hella Big Scarf.

## YARN

Woolly Mahoosive Gianto Merino (2.2 pounds [1 kg], yardage varies, 19.5-micron superfine merino, roving style yarn):

- 1 ball Pink Mushroom

## GAUGE

In stockinette st, 3 sts = 6 inches (15 cm) and 2 rows = 4 inches (10 cm). To save time, take time to check gauge.

## FINISHED MEASUREMENTS

28 x 84 inches (71 x 213 cm)

## NEEDLES

Your arms! Or US 50 (25-mm) straight needles, or size needed to obtain correct gauge

## NOTIONS

Your fingers! Or 25-mm crochet hook for weaving in ends

## TECHNIQUE

Arm Knitting (page 109)

## NOW LET'S GET ARM KNITTING!

CO 8 sts

ROWS 1–2: K across.

ROW 3: P across.

ROWS 4–5: K across.

ROW 6: P across.

ROWS 7–11: K across.

ROW 12: P across.

ROWS 13–17: K across.

ROW 18: P across.

ROWS 19–23: K across.

ROW 24: P across.

ROWS 25–29: K across.

ROW 30: P across.

(CONTINUED)

ROWS 31-35: K across.

ROW 36: P across.

ROWS 37-38: K across.

ROW 39: P across.

ROW 40-41: K across.

## FINISHING

BO as you would for a normal scarf: K2, then slip the first st over the second and off your arm. When you've finished binding off, you can use your fingers to tuck the ends of the wool into the scarf.

Wear your hella big scarf around town or cuddle up on the couch with it!

# LENNY SCARF

Yum, brioche! I love a good French pastry. Whoops, wrong brioche! Brioche knitting creates a beautifully textured, extra cozy fabric. As we are already using extra cozy yarn, this pattern features the half brioche stitch in sections, keeping the extra weight to a minimum.

If you've never attempted brioche knitting, head to the Techniques section on page 115 to find a step-by-step guide on this intricate looking yet attainable stitch. Brioche knitting involves slipped stitches, creating an extra layer of knitting. On the right side of the work, you'll see a raised column of knits creating elevated texture. On the wrong side of the work, it will almost look like a column is missing.

I designed this scarf in an effort to simplify brioche. Complex stitches often feel daunting to a beginner or even intermediate knitter! By using a yarn that is bulkier, you will be able to spot the differences between the yarn overs (YOs) and regular knit stitches.

## YARN
Wool and the Gang Crazy Sexy Wool
(7 ounces [200 g], 87 yards [80 m] 100% wool):

- 3 balls Curasao Blue

## GAUGE
In garter st, 6 sts and 12 rows = 4 inches (10 cm). To save time, take time to check gauge.

## FINISHED MEASUREMENTS
10 x 76 inches (25 x 193 cm)

## NEEDLES
US 19 (15-mm) straight or circular needles, or size needed to obtain correct gauge

## NOTIONS
6 stitch markers. While not required, I recommend using stitch markers to note where the brioche sections stop and start.

Darning needle or 15-mm crochet hook for weaving in ends

## TECHNIQUES
Garter Stitch (page 115)

Half Brioche Stitch (page 115)

## NOW LET'S GET KNITTING!
CO 17 sts.

ROWS 1–4: K across.

ROW 5: K3, k1, yfwd, sl1yo, yb, k1, k11.

ROW 6: K11, p1, BRK, p1, k3.

ROWS 7–16: Rep rows 5 and 6 five more times.

ROWS 17–20: K across.

ROW 21: K7, k1, yfwd, sl1yo, yb, k1, k4.

ROW 22: K4, p1, BRK, p1, k8.

ROWS 23–32: Rep rows 5 and 6 five more times.

ROWS 33–36: K across.

ROW 37: K11, pm, k1, yfwd, sl1yo, yb, k1, k3.

ROW 38: K3, p1, BRK, p1, k9.

ROWS 39–48: Rep rows 5 and 6 five more times.

ROWS 49–192: Rep rows 1–48 three more times.

ROWS 193–196: K across.

## FINISHING
BO loosely.

WEAVE IN your ends and you're done!

# NANAY'S SCARF

This one is for all the moms out there! Whether you're 25 or 45, this scarf is functional and fashionable! Never worry about your scarf falling off when chasing your little ones around. Nanay, by the way, means "mother" in Tagalog, a Filipino dialect and my mom's native tongue.

This pattern features the double moss stitch, creating a textural landscape of diagonal columns. You will learn how to cast off mid-row, creating a slit for you to tuck the scarf in. Why, you might ask? So it never falls off! Look ma, no hands!

## YARN
Wool and the Gang Crazy Sexy Wool (7 ounces [200 g], 87 yards [80 m] 100% wool):

- 3 balls Funfetti Latte

## GAUGE
In double moss st, 6 sts and 8 rows = 4 inches (10 cm). To save time, take time to check gauge.

## FINISHED MEASUREMENTS
8 x 56 inches (20 x 142 cm)

## NEEDLES
US 19 (15-mm) straight or circular needles, or size needed to obtain correct gauge

## NOTIONS
Darning needle or crochet hook for weaving in ends

## TECHNIQUE
Double Moss Stitch (page 115)

## DESIGNER NOTE
To create a clean edge, slip the 1st st of every row.

## NOW LET'S GET KNITTING!
CO 13 sts.

ROWS 1–4: Following the steps on page 115 k the double moss stitch pattern.

ROWS 5–78: Rep double moss stitch 18 times, ending with Row 2.

## CENTER SLIT SECTION
ROW 79: K6, BO1, k6. You now have two separate panels, 6 sts on each side. Continue to k on both sides for each row with separate balls of yarn.

ROWS 80–89: Working the two sides separately, k in double moss stitch.

## FINAL SECTION
ROW 90: K6, CO1, k6 with same yarn, joining the two panels.

ROWS 91–120: Work double moss stitch pattern 16 times.

## FINISHING
BO in pattern.

WEAVE IN all ends, using the tails from where you joined new balls of yarn to reinforce the connection.

# COWLS

QUICK INFINITY-STYLE SCARVES FOR MOVERS, SHAKERS AND DO-ERS

# COWLS ARE THE PERFECT WEEKEND PROJECT;

knit them up and show your work off the same day! Most of these cowls are infinity-style scarves. They wrap once or twice around your neck, creating a barrier from harsh winds.

With no ends, you're free to move about how you please, knowing the cowl will never fall off or be in your way! Grab your cowl if you're always on the go and need to keep your neck and face warm.

This chapter will feature two ways to knit a cowl: in the round or by seaming up the sides. If you're knitting a scarf in the round, like the Cascades Cowl (page 44), bulky yarn will allow you to be quick in creating both a fashionable but functional piece. When seaming, like in the Clark Cowl (page 48), the magnified stitches will allow you to clearly line up the proper stitches, creating an even and neat seam. Some feature textures, like the Rhaye Cowl (page 43) and the Morrison Cowl (page 51), while others, such as the Radius Hooded Cowl (page 55), might teach you more about construction. Whichever cowl you choose, you'll be done within a weekend, if not one sitting!

# RHAYE COWL

The Rhaye Cowl is a warm and modern cowl that offers versatility because you can wear it around your neck or like a hoodie! It makes a great pop of color and texture to any outfit and keeps you snuggly on the go—what could be better?

By using the thinner but still jumbo needle size US 17 (12.5 mm), I've found that the texture of the pattern, otherwise known as the basketweave stitch, pops more but still allows drape for when you wear it as a hoodie. The pattern is a simple repetition of knits and purls in sectioned blocks, allowing you to do a bit of autopilot knitting.

The Rhaye Cowl is one of the quicker knit patterns found in my book, making for a quick gift or simply a satisfying project on a free afternoon. The absolute best part? You don't have to seam the ends together because it's knit in the round!

## YARN

Wool and the Gang Crazy Sexy Wool
(7 ounces [200 g], 87 yards [80 m] 100% wool):

- 2 balls Mellow Mauve

## GAUGE

In basketweave pattern, 6.5 sts and 9.25 rnds = 4 inches (10 cm). To save time, take time to check gauge.

## FINISHED MEASUREMENTS

31-inch (79-cm) circumference, 13 inches (33 cm) tall

## NEEDLES

US 17 (12.5-mm) 24- or 29-inch (61- or 74-cm) circular needles, or size needed to obtain correct gauge

## NOTIONS

Stitch marker or scrap yarn to mark the beginning of the round

12-mm crochet hook for weaving in ends

## TECHNIQUES

Join in the Round (page 119)

Basketweave Pattern (page 111)

## NOW LET'S GET KNITTING!

CO 50 sts. Join in the round, being careful not to twist the sts; pm.

RNDS 1-30: Work the basket weave pattern three times.

## FINISHING

BO loosely in pattern (knitting the knits and purling the purls). Don't forget to remove your marker!

WEAVE IN your ends and boom! Your Rhaye Cowl is ready to wear!

# CASCADES COWL

The Cascades Cowl is another combo of knits and purls but needs a little more attention. Worked up in alternating rows, a textured landscape is created mimicking the peaks of the Pacific Northwest. Similar to the Rhaye Cowl (page 43), the Cascades Cowl will take you roughly 1½ to 2 hours, another perfect quick gift pattern. This cowl can be worn around the neck or as a shoulder shrug, but not so much as a hoodie. This would be great for the commuter in your family, keeping them warm on a bike ride or walk into work.

The stitch featured in this cowl is referred to as the mistake rib. Its first row starts as a classic rib: alternating between purls and knits. The real fun comes in the second row, off-setting the repeat pattern by one. Getting lost? Don't worry, it will make sense as we get started.

## YARN

Wool and the Gang Crazy Sexy Wool
(7 ounces [200 g], 87 yards [80 m] 100% wool):

- 2 balls Salt and Pepper

## GAUGE

In mistake rib, 6.5 sts and 9.5 rows = 4 inches (10 cm). To save time, take time to check gauge.

## FINISHED MEASUREMENTS

34-inch (86-cm) circumference, 12 inches (30 cm) tall

## NEEDLES

US 17 (12.5-mm) 24- or 29-inch (61- or 74-cm) circular needles, or size needed to obtain correct gauge

## NOTIONS

Stitch marker or scrap yarn to mark the beginning of the round

Darning needle or crochet hook for weaving in ends

## TECHNIQUES

Alternate Rib Cast On (page 111)

Join in the Round (page 119)

Mistake Rib (page 121)

## NOW LET'S GET KNITTING!

CO 56 sts. Join in the round, being careful not to twist the sts, pm.

RNDS 1-28: Work in mistake rib pattern for 28 rnds (12 inches [30 cm]) or until desired length.

## FINISHING

BO loosely in pattern (knitting the knits and purling the purls). Don't forget to remove your marker!

BEFORE weaving in your ends, turn the cowl inside out. I have found the "wrong side" of the work looks slightly more defined than the "right side" of the work. Weave in your ends.

# LA TORTUGA COWL

Growing up, I learned Spanish and English simultaneously. Being able to speak both languages has allowed me to navigate different worlds within each culture. As a result, I can make this craft more accessible and spread the joy of creating something with your own two hands. Tortuga is Spanish for turtle, and just like a turtle's shell, this cowl is constructed to make the perfect barrier from danger, or cold!

La Tortuga Cowl is your classic cowl: it sticks close around your neck for warmth but is drapey enough that it lays nicely against your chest. This cowl came about when I had leftover yarn from other projects. The middle of the design features a pop of color, needing only a few yards of yarn. Therefore, it is a perfect stash buster if you have some leftover chunky wool.

## YARN

Wool and the Gang Crazy Sexy Wool
(7 ounces [200 g], 87 yards [80 m] 100% wool):

- 2 balls Salt and Pepper (Color A)
- 1 ball Duck Egg Blue (Color B)

## GAUGE

With larger needles in garter st, 6 sts and 12 rnds = 4 inches (10 cm). To save time, take time to check gauge.

## FINISHED MEASUREMENTS

33-inch (84-cm) circumference, 10 inches (25 cm) tall

## NEEDLES

US 17 (12.5-mm) 29-inch (74-cm) circular needles and US 19 (15-mm) 29-inch (74-cm) circular needles, or sizes needed to obtain correct gauge

## NOTIONS

Stitch marker or scrap yarn to mark the beginning of the round

Darning needle or crochet hook for weaving in ends

## TECHNIQUES

Garter Stitch (page 115)

Join in the Round (page 119)

## NOW LET'S GET KNITTING!

WITH COLOR A AND SMALLER NEEDLES, CO 50 sts. Join into rnd being careful not to twist the sts, pm.

RNDS 1-5: *K1tbl, p1; rep from * around.

SWITCH to larger needles.

RND 6: K around.

RND 7: P around.

RND 8: Join Color B and k around.

RND 9: With Color A, p around.

RND 10: With Color B, k around.

RNDS 11-18: Rep rnds 9 and 10 four more times.

RND 19: Cut Color B. With Color A, p around.

RND 20: With Color A, k around.

RND 21: P around.

SWITCH back to smaller needles.

RNDS 22-26: * K1tbl, p1; rep from * around.

## FINISHING

BO in pattern, knitting the knits and purling the purls. Weave in all ends.

# CLARK COWL

The Clark Cowl offers bold patches of color and features the simple garter stitch.

In 2016, I entered my first two-day craft show. As I've mentioned before, I'm a procrasti-knitter. I needed lots of scarves fast and there isn't a stitch easier than garter stitch, but plain one-color scarves sounded so boring to me. Out came the Clark Cowl, whose bold color changes but simple stitching allowed me to prep fairly quickly for the market. Hopefully, it can help you knit cowls for the whole family in a week!

Unlike the other cowls in this section, this cowl is worked flat and then seamed using the Horizontal Invisible Seam Stitch. I've demonstrated this technique on page 117 using contrasting colors to highlight where you should be inserting your needle.

## YARN

Wool and the Gang Crazy Sexy Wool
(7 ounces [200 g], 87 yards [80 m] 100% wool):

- 1 ball Eagle Grey (Color A)
- 1 ball Cameo Rose (Color B)
- 1 ball Cinnamon Dust (Color C)

## GAUGE

In garter stitch, 6 sts and 12 rows = 4 inches (10 cm). To save time, take time to check gauge.

## FINISHED MEASUREMENTS

14 inches (35.5 cm) wide, 23-inch (58-cm) circumference

## NEEDLES

US 19 (15-mm) straight or circular needles, or size needed to obtain correct gauge

## NOTIONS

Darning needle or crochet hook for weaving in ends and seaming

## TECHNIQUES

Garter Stitch (page 115)

Horizontal Invisible Seam Stitch (page 117)

## NOW LET'S GET KNITTING!

USING COLOR A, CO 21 sts.

ROWS 1–14: K.

ROW 15: Cut Color A, leaving enough tail to weave in later. Join Color B, k across.

ROWS 16–20: K across.

ROW 21: Cut Color B, leaving enough tail to weave in later. Join Color C, k across.

ROWS 22–26: K across.

ROW 27: Cut Color C, leaving enough tail to weave in later. Join Color A, k across.

ROWS 28–36: K across.

## FINISHING

BO loosely in Color A.

TAKING your darning needle and about 30 inches (76 cm) of Color A, seam the cast-on and bind-off edges together using the horizontal seam stitch.

WEAVE IN your ends and enjoy!

# MORRISON COWL

Although two-color brioche may look intimidating, it is nothing more than a series of knits, purls and yarn overs. For the brioche beginner who is looking to advance, the Morrison Cowl is the way to go! The entire cowl is knit up in two colors, making it easy to determine which stitches to k and p together.

Using Woolfolk Hygge, a yarn that falls under the "Super Bulky" category, the Morrison Cowl knits up in a few hours. The yarn's chain-like structure allows the scarf to be drapey and airy but still strong against a winter storm.

## YARN

Woolfolk Hygge (76 yards [70 m], 3.5 ounces [100 g], 50% Ovis 21 Ultimate Merino®, 28% superbaby alpaca, 22% mulberry silk):

- 1 skein Navy (Color A)
- 1 skein Silver Grey (Color B)

## GAUGE

In brioche st, 3 sts and 6.25 rnds = 4 inches (10 cm). This pattern is not overly dependent on gauge.

## FINISHED MEASUREMENTS

60-inch (152-cm) circumference, 7 inches (18 cm) tall

## NEEDLES

US 17 (12.5 mm) 40-inch (102-cm) circular needles, or size needed to obtain correct gauge

## NOTIONS

Stitch marker or scrap yarn to mark the beg of the round

Darning needle or crochet hook for weaving in ends

## TECHNIQUES

Join in the Round (page 119)

Brioche (page 112)

## NOW LET'S GET KNITTING!

USING COLOR A, CO 80 sts. Join in the round, being careful not to twist the sts; pm.

RND 1 (SET-UP ROUND): With Color A, *yfwd, sl1yo, k1; rep from * around.

RND 2: With Color B, *BRP, sl1yo; rep from * around.

RND 3: With Color A, *yfwd, sl1yo, BRK; rep from * around.

REP Rnds 2 and 3 ten times. You will be alternating colors each round (Color A for odd rounds and Color B for even rounds). You should end with Color B.

## FINISHING

BO in pattern using Color A.

WEAVE IN all ends. (There should only be the CO and BO tails to weave in.)

# CHELSEA ARM KNIT COWL

The Chelsea Arm Knit Cowl feels like what a cloud should. It's soft, fluffy and a little dense. Knitting the Chelsea gives you just a taste of the technique by using a smaller quantity of yarn than a blanket would need, therefore saving you time and money. If you have always wanted to try arm knitting but don't want to throw down a large chunk of money on a blanket's worth of yarn, the Chelsea Arm Knit Cowl is the perfect alternative.

The Chelsea also utilizes an alternate style of arm knitting. You still use your arms but instead of your arms as the needles, you lay your work out flat in front of you. Head to the Techniques section (page 110) for step-by-step instructions.

## YARN
Woolly Mahoosive Squiggly (2.2 pounds [1 kg], yardage varies, 19.5 micron superfine merino roving style yarn):

- 1 ball.Light Grey

## GAUGE
In stockinette st, 2 sts and 2 rows = 4 inches (10 cm). To save time, take time to check gauge.

## FINISHED MEASUREMENTS
9 inches (23 cm) wide, 28-inch (71-cm) circumference

## NEEDLES
Your arms! Or US 50 (25-mm) straight needles, or size needed to obtain correct gauge

## NOTIONS
Your fingers! Or 25-mm crochet hook for weaving in ends and sewing seam

## TECHNIQUES
Stockinette Stitch (page 123)

Arm Knitting—alternate technique (page 110)

Horizontal Invisible Seam Stitch (page 117)

## NOW LET'S GET ARM KNITTING!
CO 8 sts.

ROWS 1–2: K.

ROW 3: P.

REP rows 1–3 until your work measures 28 inches (71 cm).

## FINISHING
BO. Use the horizontal invisible seam stitch to join the CO and BO edges. Weave in all ends.

# RADIUS HOODED COWL

Traditionally, a cowl has a large loose head. This hooded cowl is the truest to that definition. It is constructed to lay around your neck but can spread around your shoulders. It also has a hood for those extra cold days. It reminds me a little of a Dementor's cloak but sturdier.

Starting in the round, this scarf features brioche ridges followed up with some flat knitting. To complete the look, the top edges are seamed together. Whether you use it for function, cosplay, or both, I hope you enjoy this woolly construction!

## YARN

Wool and the Gang Crazy Sexy Wool (7 ounces [200 g], 87 yards [80 m] 100% wool):

- 2 balls Rocky Grey

## GAUGE

In stockinette st, 6 sts and 10 rows = 4 inches (10 cm). This pattern is not overly dependent on gauge.

## FINISHED MEASUREMENTS

37-inch (94-cm) circumference

## NEEDLES

US 17 (12.5-mm) 40-inch (102-cm) circular needles, or size needed to obtain correct gauge

## NOTIONS

Stitch marker or scrap yarn to mark the beginning of the round

US 17 (12.5-mm) cable needle (or another set of US 17 [12.5-mm] circular needles)

Darning needle or crochet hook for weaving in ends

## TECHNIQUES

Stockinette Stitch (page 123)

Join in the Round (page 119)

Brioche (page 112)

3-Needle Bind Off (page 124)

## NOW LET'S GET KNITTING!

CO 56 sts. Join in the round, being careful not to twist the sts, pm.

RNDS 1–3: *K1, p1; rep from * around. This is known as a 1x1 rib stitch.

RND 4 (PREP RND): *P7, (p1, sl1yo) three times, p1; rep from * around.

RND 5: *P7, (p1, sl1yo) three times, p1; rep from * around.

RND 6: *P7, (*p1, BRK) three times, p1; rep from * around.

RNDS 7–24: Rep rnds 5 and 6 nine more times.

## HOOD

You will now knit flat.

ROW 1 (RS): P4, BO14 in purl, p4, continue in pattern to EOR (42 sts). Rm.

ROW 2 (WS): K5, *(BRP, k1) twice, BRP, k9; rep from * to 9 sts before end (BRP, k1) twice, BRP, k4.

ROW 3 (RS): P4, *(sl1yo, p1) twice, sl1yo, p9; rep from * to 10 sts before end (sl1yo, p1) twice, sl1yo, p5.

ROWS 4–27: Rep rows 2 and 3 twelve more times.

ROW 28: Rep row 2.

(CONTINUED)

ROW 33: P4, (sl1yo, p1) twice, sl1yo, p5, p2tog, (sl1yo, p1) twice, sl1yo, p2togtbl, p5, (sl1yo, p1) twice, sl1yo, p5.

ROW 34: K5, *(BRP, k1) twice, BRP, k6; rep from * to 9 sts before end (BRP, k1) twice, BRP, k4.

ROW 35: P4, (sl1yo, p1) twice, sl1yo, p4, p2tog, (sl1yo, p1) twice, sl1yo, p2togtbl, p4, (sl1yo, p1) twice, sl1yo, p5.

ROW 36: K5, *(BRP, k1) twice, BRP, k7; rep from * to 9 sts before end (BRP, k1) twice, BRP, k4.

DECREASE every row as follows:

ROW 37: P4, (sl1yo, p1) twice, sl1yo, p3, p2tog, (sl1yo, p1) twice, sl1yo, p2togtbl, p3, (sl1yo, p1) twice, sl1yo, p5.

ROW 38: K5, (BRP, k1) twice, BRP, k2, ssk, (BRP, k1) twice, BRP, k2tog, k2, (BRP, k1) twice, BRP, k4.

ROW 39: P4, (sl1yo, p1) twice, sl1yo, p1, p2tog, (sl1yo, p1) twice, sl1yo, p2togtbl, p1, (sl1yo, p1) twice, sl1yo, p5.

ROW 40: K3, k2tog, (BRP, k1) twice, BRP, ssk, (BRP, k1) twice, BRP, k2tog, (BRP, k1) twice, BRP, k4.

## FINISHING

FOLD hood in half with RS together. BO using 3-needle bind off (you will have one unmatched stitch at center back, BO as normal for this last st).

WEAVE IN ends.

## CROWN

DECREASE every other row as follows:

ROW 29: P4, (sl1yo, p1) twice, sl1yo, p7, p2tog, (sl1yo, p1) twice, sl1yo, p2togtbl, p7, (sl1yo, p1) twice, sl1yo, p5.

ROW 30: K5, *(BRP, k1) twice, BRP, k8; rep from * to 9 sts before end (BRP, k1) twice, BRP, k4.

ROW 31: P4, (sl1yo, p1) twice, sl1yo, p6, p2tog, (sl1yo, p1) twice, sl1yo, p2togtbl, p6, (sl1yo, p1) twice, sl1yo, p5.

ROW 32: K5, *(BRP, k1) twice, BRP, k7; rep from * to 9 sts before end (BRP, k1) twice, BRP, k4.

# BEANIES

FROM SKULLCAPS TO EARFLAPS, HATS FOR THE WHOLE FAMILY

**WHO DOESN'T LOVE A GOOD BEANIE?** Whether you're actually cold, having a bad hair day or just live in Portland, Oregon, where it is mandatory every resident wear one (hah!), beanies are utilitarian but also a fashion staple.

In this chapter, I'll cover every beanie, from a classic rib to ear flaps. Although there is a bit of construction involved, almost all of these beanies are suitable for all levels. For the Casual Knitter waiting to put all the skills they've learned to good use, for the Adventurous Knitter ready to learn new skills and even for the Granny-Level Knitter who has knit everything under the sun but needs a quick birthday gift.

This chapter also features the thinner end of the chunky spectrum. These yarns are still considered bulky according the Standard Yarn Weight System. As I started out with mostly chunky yarn, these thinner bulky yarns were the perfect transition between chunky and worsted weights. They are still bulky so they work up quickly, but they offer more drape as they aren't as thick. Likewise, if you've strictly only used Aran or worsted weights, the bulky yarn is a good introduction to bigger yarns. They aren't super bulky like Hygge, the yarn used in the Morrison Cowl (page 51), but you can still knit up a hat within a weekend! To check out these yarns, try Don's Night Cap (page 74) or Miss Van's Balaclava (page 70).

# MULTNOMAH BEANIE

When I asked my friends and family what they thought of this beanie, I got very mixed reviews: "It just looks weird" vs. "I'm into it!" That's when it hit me. Weird isn't always bad. After all . . . We want to Keep Portland Weird.

Some might think this beanie is inside-out. In classic colorwork knitting, floats refer to the strands of yarn that run behind your work allowing you to change colors midrow. This beanie's "floats" are on the outside.

This hat is also the bulkiest in the book, featuring the "super bulky" Crazy Sexy Wool. It's great as a fashion statement or while you're snowboarding down Mt. Hood.

## YARN

Wool and the Gang Crazy Sexy Wool
(7 ounces [200 g], 87 yards [80 m] 100% wool):

- 1 ball Eagle Grey (Color A)
- 1 ball Cameo Rose (Color B)
- 1 ball Cinnamon Dust (Color C)

## GAUGE

In twisted rib, 7 sts and 10 rows = 4 inches (10 cm).

Your floats should measure approximately 2–2¼ inches (5–6 cm).

To save time, take time to check gauge.

## FINISHED MEASUREMENTS

22-inch (56-cm) circumference

## NEEDLES

US 17 (12.5-mm) 24-inch (61-cm) circular needles, or size needed to obtain correct gauge

## NOTIONS

Stitch marker or scrap yarn to mark the beginning of the round

Darning needle or crochet hook for weaving in ends

3-inch (7.6-cm) pompom maker (I like to use one by Clover)

## TECHNIQUES

Join in the Round (page 119)

Twisted Rib (page 124)

Colorful Linen Stitch (page 114)

## DESIGNER NOTE

For a snugger brim, CO 38 sts. Complete rnds 1–5 as written below. After you've attached Color B in rnd 6, using Color A k1, m1l, k1, m1l. You will now have the 40 sts. Continue following the pattern as written for rnds 6–16.

## NOW LET'S GET KNITTING!

USING COLOR A, CO 40 sts. Join in the rnd, being careful not to twist stitches.

RNDS 1–5: Work in twisted rib pattern.

RNDS 6–16: Attach Color B and work in colorful linen stitch: *Switch colors (yb Color A, yfwd Color B), k4 Color A, switch colors (yb Color B, yfwd Color A), k4 Color B; rep from * around. Rep for every rnd.

(CONTINUED)

## CROWN

KEEP WORKING each st with the same color as the prev rnd, now holding the non-working yarn to the back of the work.

RND 17: *K2tog, k2; rep from * around.

RND 18: K around.

RND 19: *K2tog, k1; rep from * around.

RND 20: K2tog around.

CUT your yarn, leaving a 12-inch (30-cm) tail. Thread your darning needle onto the tail and then through the rem sts on the needles. Remove your needles from the sts and cinch tight.

## POMPOM

SET your beanie aside to make your pompom using the pompom maker. Feel free to use only one or both of the colors you used to knit the beanie. I used a completely different color (Color C) for an extra pop.

USE the darning needle and rem tail to attach your pompom to your beanie, weaving the ends into the inside of the beanie.

FLIP your beanie inside out to tie the pompom onto the beanie, including the beanie's bind-off tail.

WEAVE IN ends. Flip outside in!

# PNW BEANIE

The PNW Beanie comes with a little extra warmth: earflaps! Its vintage design slightly resembles leather football helmets from the 1920s. Using Crazy Sexy Wool with smaller needles than those typically suggested for this yarn weight, you'll create a snug hat that can be worn by child or adult. The hat is worked in the round and the ear flaps are knit by picking up stitches from the cast-on edge.

## YARN

Wool and the Gang Crazy Sexy Wool
(7 ounces [200 g], 87 yards [80 m] 100% wool):

- 1 ball Cinnamon Dust (Color A)
- 1 ball Bronzed Olive (Color B)

## GAUGE

In garter st, 6.5 sts and 12 rows = 4 inches
(10 cm). To save time, take time to check gauge.

## FINISHED MEASUREMENTS

19½-inch (50-cm) circumference

## NEEDLES

US 15 (10-mm) 24-inch (61-cm) circular needles and matching DPNs, or size needed to obtain correct gauge

## NOTIONS

Stitch marker or scrap yarn to mark the beginning of the round

Darning needle or crochet hook for weaving in ends

## TECHNIQUES

Garter Stitch (page 115)

Join in the Round (page 119)

## NOW LET'S GET KNITTING!

CO 32 sts using Color A. Join into rnd, being careful not to twist the sts, pm.

RND 1: P around.

RND 2: K around.

RND 3: P around.

RND 4: With Color A, k1. Attach Color B and k around.

RNDS 5, 7 AND 9: With Color B, p1. With Color A, p around.

RNDS 6, 8 AND 10: With Color A, k1. With Color B, k around.

RND 11: With Color B, p around.

CUT Color A, leaving a tail long enough to weave in later.

CONTINUE pattern with Color B.

RND 12: K around.

## TRIANGLE SECTION

RND 13: *K1, p7; rep from * around.

RND 14 AND ALL EVEN ROUNDS IN TRIANGLE SECTION: K around.

RND 15: *K2, p5, k1; rep from * around.

RND 17: *K3, p3, k2; rep from * around.

RND 19: *K4, p1, k3; rep from * around.

RND 21: K around.

(CONTINUED)

## CROWN

When it becomes uncomfortable to knit with the circular needles, switch to using DPNs.

RND 22: *K2tog, k2; rep from * around.

RND 23: *K2tog, K1; rep from * around.

RND 24: *K2tog; rep from * around.

CUT your yarn, leaving a 12-inch (30-cm) tail. Thread your needle through the rem sts on the needles. Remove your needles from the sts and cinch tight.

## LEFT EARFLAP

WORKING from your CO edge, pick up 6 sts with Color A starting at 3 inches (7.5 cm) to the left of the BOR.

WORK in garter st for 3 inches (7.5 cm) (approximately 9 rows).

BO.

## RIGHT EARFLAP

WORKING from your CO edge, pick up 6 sts with Color A starting at 3 inches (7.5 cm) to the right of the BOR.

WORK in garter st (knit every row) for 3 inches (7.5 cm) (approximately 9 rows).

BO. Weave in ends.

# CADA DÍA BEANIE

This pattern is perfect for those who have only used chunky yarns in the past and are looking to move towards lighter weights. It utilizes yarns that still fall under the bulky range but are thinner and less cumbersome to carry around.

Like every knitter on earth, I wanted to design an everyday beanie. Rain or shine, bad hair day or simply being lazy—this was the beanie. Plymouth Yarn's Viento is a lightweight yarn but still falls under the "bulky" category. Not to mention it is incredibly soft! Its chain-like construction is breathable and won't leave you sweaty from wearing it all day.

## YARN

Plymouth Yarn Viento (1¾ ounces [50 g], 98 yards [90 m] 70% baby alpaca, 30% bamboo):

- 1 skein #2 Medium Grey

## GAUGE

In twisted rib, 11 sts and 14 rows = 4 inches (10 cm), without stretching. To save time, take time to check gauge.

## FINISHED MEASUREMENTS

18-inch (46-cm) circumference, unstretched

## NEEDLES

US 15 (10-mm) 16-inch (41-cm) circular needles and matching DPNs, or size needed to obtain correct gauge

## NOTIONS

Stitch marker or scrap yarn to mark the beginning of the round

Darning needle or crochet hook for weaving in ends

## TECHNIQUES

Alternate Ribbing Cast On (page 111)

Join in the Round (page 119)

Twisted Rib (page 124)

## NOW LET'S GET KNITTING!

CO 50 sts using the alternate ribbing cast on. Join into rnd, being careful not to twist the sts, pm.

## BODY

RNDS 1–30: Work twisted rib pattern for 30 rnds.

## CROWN

RND 31: *K2tog, work 3 sts in pattern; rep from * around. This means you knit the ks and purl the ps. Be sure to continue working through the back loop.

RND 32: Work around, in pattern.

RND 33: *K2tog, work 2 in pattern; rep from * around.

RND 34: *K2tog, work 1 in pattern; rep from * around.

RND 35: K2tog around.

RND 36: K2tog around.

## FINISHING

CUT your yarn, leaving a 12-inch (30-cm) tail. Thread your needle through the rem sts on the needles. Remove your needles from the sts and cinch tight. Flip the beanie inside out, poking the darning needle with the yarn through the center of the cinch. Tie a tight knot and weave the rest of the tail into your beanie. Flip the beanie outside out and you're done!

# MISS VAN'S BALACLAVA

This pattern is all about construction. If you're looking for a technical challenge, Miss Van's Balaclava is for you! It features knitting in the round, the herringbone stitch and decreases. Challenge yourself with this modern ski mask!

Have you ever seen a mural by Miss Van? Put down my book right now and Google Miss Van, I'll wait. Whoooaaa, right?! Her murals hit you with bold colors and a velvety texture. Her masked murals inspired this fun design.

In this pattern, you'll begin by knitting in the round. I highlight a proper twisted rib, knitting through the back loop of both the knits and purls, giving the section around your neck a defined texture. The rib also allows for stretch.

The herringbone portion is knit flat. In order to make a hole for your face, you'll learn how to bind off mid-round, knit flat for a number of rows and then cast on mid-round. This is followed by decrease shaping for the top of your head. I like to think of this pattern as a knitting puzzle, keeping your attention with every stitch.

## YARN

Sugarbush Dawson (3½ ounces [100 g], 165 yards [150 m], 50% llama soft, 50% merino wool):

- 1 skein #1307 Babbling Brook

## GAUGE

In twisted rib, 11 sts and 14 rows = 4 inches (10 cm), without stretching. To save time, take time to check gauge.

## FINISHED MEASUREMENTS

22-inch (56-cm) circumference, 14 inches (35.5 cm) long

## NEEDLES

US 15 (10-mm) 16-inch (41-cm) circular needles and matching DPNs, or size needed to obtain correct gauge

## NOTIONS

2 stitch markers or scrap yarn

Darning needle or crochet hook for weaving in ends

## TECHNIQUES

Herringbone Stitch (page 117)

Twisted Rib (page 124)

## DESIGNER NOTE

The ribbed fabric is very stretchy and we want a snug fit, so although the balaclava may look too small while you are working on it, you'll be surprised at how well this fits most folks!

## NOW LET'S GET KNITTING!

CO 60 sts. Join in the rnd, being careful not to twist the sts, pm.

## NECK

RNDS 1-28: Work in twisted rib (approx. 8 inches [20 cm] or as long as needed).

## FACE

RND 29: Work in twisted rib until 14 sts rem on needle. BO 14 sts (46 sts rem).

ROWS 30-36: Work in herringbone st (flat) for 7 rows.

(CONTINUED)

## FOREHEAD

CO 14, pm, join back into rnd, being careful not to twist the sts. This is your BOR marker.

RND 37: K46, pm, work 14 sts in twisted rib (over the CO sts). The markers highlight the twisted rib section above the forehead.

RNDS 38-39: Rep last rnd 2 more times. Remove the second marker during rnd 39.

## CROWN

SWITCH to DPNs when knitting with circular needles becomes uncomfortable.

RND 40: *K4, k2tog; rep from * around (50 sts rem).

RND 41: K.

RND 42: *K3, k2tog; rep from * around (40 sts rem).

RND 43: K.

RND 44: *K2, k2tog; rep from * around (30 sts rem).

RND 45: K.

RND 46: *K1, k2tog; rep from * around (20 sts rem).

RND 47: K.

RND 48: K2tog around (10 sts rem).

RND 49: K2tog around (5 sts rem). Rm.

## FINISHING

CUT a 12-inch (30-cm) tail and weave it through the leftover sts on the needle. Cinch tight and weave in ends!

# DON'S NIGHT CAP

Using a combination of classic stitches, this hat knits up as a modern skullcap. Made with a bulky but not too heavy yarn, this beanie is perfect to wear during a late summer night on the beach or a brisk fall morning running errands.

## YARN

Brooklyn Tweed Quarry (3½ ounces [100 g], 200 yards [183 m], 100% Wyoming-grown Targhee-Columbia wool):

- 1 skein Hematite

## GAUGE

In linen st, 12 sts and 10 rows = 4 inches (10 cm). To save time, take time to check gauge.

## FINISHED MEASUREMENTS

20-inch (51-cm) circumference, 6 inches (15 cm) tall

## NEEDLES

US 15 (10-mm) 16-inch (41-cm) circular needles and matching DPNs, or size needed to obtain correct gauge

## NOTIONS

Stitch marker or scrap yarn to mark the beginning of the rnd

Darning needle or crochet hook for weaving in ends

## TECHNIQUES

Join in the Round (page 119)

Twisted Rib (page 124)

## NOW LET'S GET KNITTING!

CO 50 sts. Join in the rnd, being careful not to twist the sts; pm.

RNDS 1–4: Work in twisted rib for 4 rnds.

RND 5: * Knit in twisted rib for 5 sts, m1l; rep from * around until last 5 sts. Knit in twisted rib. (59 sts.)

RND 6: *K1, sl1wyif; rep from * around until last stitch. K1.

RND 7: *Sl1wyif, k1; rep from * around until last stitch. Sl1wyif.

RNDS 8–25: Rnds 6 and 7 create the linen stitch pattern. Continue repeating rnds 6 and 7 for 18 rnds or your desired length. On the last rnd, M1L one st before the marker (60 sts).

## CROWN

SWITCH to DPNs when knitting with circular needles becomes uncomfortable.

RND 26: *K4, k2tog; rep from * around (50 sts rem).

RND 27: K.

RND 28: *K3, k2tog; rep from * around (40 sts rem).

RND 29: K.

RND 30: *K2, k2tog; rep from * around (30 sts rem).

RND 31: K.

RND 32: *K1, k2tog; rep from * around (20 sts rem).

RND 33: K2tog around (10 sts rem).

## FINISHING

CUT your yarn, leaving a 12-inch (30-cm) tail. Thread your darning needle onto the tail and then through the rem sts on the needles. Remove your needles from the sts and cinch tight.

WEAVE IN ends.

# FURRY FRIENDS

## OUR PETS NEED SOME HANDMADE LOVE, TOO

## I HAVE THREE DOGS.

Yes, I said three. Winston the dorkie, Walter the corgi and Ember the mini Aussie. They make a short but mighty pack. Ember is a little skittish and Winston is camera shy, so you'll mostly see Walter in this book.

When I ventured into knitting furniture and household décor, dog beds were first on my list. Seeing my pups use what I made them with my own two hands was beyond heartwarming and affirming. Until Walter decided everything I made was his and would attempt to lie on the project well before it was finished . . .

The four patterns in this chapter are meant for your furry friends, whether they be dogs, cats, guinea pigs, tigers . . . Whatever your pet may be, he/she has something in here to use.

All patterns feature washable materials, either by machine or hand. Some of them can also be used as household staples like Winston's Mat (page 83) or Paco's Pillow (page 84). Versatility is the name of the game here, folks!

# TUG-O-WAR TOY

Puppy or old hound, this toy is for those dogs out there that love a good tug. While it uses chunky rope and not yarn, this durable chew toy will provide heaps of fun—with supervision!—for you and your best friend.

Knit as a simple I-cord, you then tie knots throughout its length, creating knobs for your pup to latch onto. If you have a playful cat, you can hang this from a doorknob so it has something to bat at.

### FIBER
Modern Macramé 5 mm 3-ply twisted rope
- 100 feet (30 m) Teal

### GAUGE
Gauge is not important for this pattern.

### FINISHED MEASUREMENTS:
Approximately 2 feet (61 cm) long

### NEEDLES
US 17 (12.5-mm) circular needles or DPNs

### TECHNIQUES
I-cord (page 118)

## NOW LET'S GET KNITTING!
CO 5 sts.

ROW 1 (I-CORD): Slide your sts to the other end of the needle. Pulling the rope from the left side of the work, k5. Make sure to pull tight on the first st, closing the I-cord.

REP row 1 until you have used up your bundle of rope, leaving some length to BO.

BO.

STARTING at one end of your knitted cord, tie the cord into a simple overhand knot. Rep overhand knot every 12 inches (30 cm). You'll end up with three knots.

PLAY tug-o-war!

# JAX SCARF

My mom also has three dogs. When I was in eighth grade, we got Tangles. Mister followed in high school. Then Jax took my place when I left for college. My mom, being a crazy dog lady like myself, wanted matching scarves for her boys, Mister and Jax. I proceeded to design a cowl that had a little opening to feed a leash through during walks.

This pattern features a twisted rib, casting off in the middle of a row and adding a stitch in the middle of a row. This allows a space for the collar and leash to meet without stretching the knitted fabric! Featuring an affordable and machine washable bulky yarn, you'll be knitting this scarf for every dog in the neighborhood!

## YARN

Lion Brand Wool Ease (6 ounces [170 g], 106 yds [97 m]), 82% acrylic/10% wool/8% rayon):

- 1 ball Denim

## GAUGE

In stockinette st, 8 sts and 11 rows = 4 inches (10 cm). To save time, take time to check gauge.

## FINISHED MEASUREMENTS

5½ inches (14 cm) wide, 7-inch (18-cm) circumference as written

## NEEDLES

US 15 (10-mm) circular or straight needles, or size needed to obtain correct gauge

## NOTIONS

Darning needle or crochet hook for weaving in ends

## TECHNIQUES

Stockinette Stitch (page 123)

Horizontal Invisible Seam Stitch (page 117)

Twisted Rib (page 124)

## NOW LET'S GET KNITTING!

CO 15 sts.

ROWS 1-14: Work in twisted rib stitch. Slip the first stitch of each row to create a neat edge.

MAKE the leash/collar hole over the next 2 rows.

ROW 15: Continue in pattern for 7 sts, BO 1, continue in pattern for 7 sts.

ROW 16: Continue in pattern for 7 sts, CO 1, continue in pattern for 7 sts.

ROWS 17-31: Work in twisted rib pattern.

CHECK if the piece is long enough to fit around your dog's neck. Continue knitting if more length is needed.

## FINISHING

BO.

SEAM CO and BO edges together using the horizontal seam stitch.

WEAVE IN all ends.

# WINSTON'S MAT

Whether you have a doggo, a cat or a guinea pig, this mat creates a nice spot for your furry friend to relax. Winston, my dachshund mix, is a lover of people, carrots and the sun. He's partially bald, so Winston will sunbathe any chance he gets. Anywhere, anytime, if you see a patch of sun, Winston is most likely sleeping in it already.

I thought it might be neat to create a mat for him and his siblings when they are laying out. It's also useful as a travel mat for long car rides or lining the inside of a crate.

Winston's Mat can be made with a few variations. Although this pattern highlights Love Fest Fibers' thick and durable Tough Love Yarn, you can also use cotton rope. Following the pattern using 3-ply 5-mm cotton rope and the US 50 (25-mm) needles will result in more of an airy, lacy-looking mat. Two strands of 5-mm cotton rope and the US 50 (25-mm) needles will give you an extra textured panel.

If you don't have any pets, this mat can be used all over the house: kitchen rug by the sink, bathroom rug by the sink, rug by the front door. You can even use it outside. If you're worried about the mat collecting too much dirt, do not fear! Love Fest Fibers' Tough Love is machine washable! Just make sure to dry it flat, preferably in the sun and perhaps with a weight (box, hamper, empty suitcase) on top to help keep the edges from curling.

## YARN
Love Fest Fibers Tough Love (25 ounces [709 g], 50 yards [46 m], 100% New Zealand wool)

- 1 ball Guava

## GAUGE
In herringbone st, 4 sts and 5 rows = 4 inches (10 cm). This pattern is not overly dependent on gauge.

## FINISHED MEASUREMENTS
20 x 18 inches (51 x 46 cm)

## NEEDLES
US 50 (25-mm) straight needles, or size needed to obtain correct gauge

## NOTIONS
25-mm crochet hook for weaving in ends

## TECHNIQUE
Herringbone Stitch (page 117)

## NOW LET'S GET KNITTING!
CO 18 sts.

ROWS 1-16: Work in Herringbone st for all 16 rows.

## FINISHING
BO. Weave in all ends.

# PACO'S PILLOW

This pillow works well for your pets, your home or both! My dog Walter loves to lie on my things. My bags, our clothes, our shoes . . . But the one thing he lies on the most? Our pillows. Since the first night we took him in, Walter has always preferred sleeping on one of our pillows.

In the summer of 2017, I went through a pillow phase. Mostly crocheted and meant to be used outside as they were made with sturdier recycled fabric yarn. But as you read in the Furry Friends intro, my dogs like to lie on my WIPs. I ended up making a pillow for our couch. Although I intended for humans to use the pillow, Walter quickly claimed it as his own.

## YARN
Loopy Mango Big Cotton (3½ ounces [100 g], 48 yards [43 m], 100% cotton):

- 5 balls Ginger

## GAUGE
In stockinette st, 7 sts and 10 rows = 4 inches (10 cm). This pattern is not overly dependent on gauge.

## FINISHED MEASUREMENTS
Fits a 20-inch (51-cm) square pillow form

## NEEDLES
US 17 (12.5-mm) 32-inch (81-cm) circular needles, or size needed to obtain correct gauge.

## NOTIONS
Darning needle or crochet hook for weaving in ends

20-inch (51-cm) square pillow insert, poly-fil or scrap yarn

## TECHNIQUES
Join in the Round (page 119)

Horizontal Invisible Seam Stitch (page 117)

## NOW LET'S GET KNITTING!
CO 68 sts. Join in the rnd, being careful not to twist the sts; pm.

RNDS 1–2: *K1, p1; rep from * around.

RNDS 3–4: *P1, k1; rep from * around.

RNDS 5–7: *K1, p1; rep from * around.

RNDS 8–10: *P1, k1; rep from * around.

REPEAT Rnds 1–10 until piece measures 20 inches (51 cm).

## FINISHING
BO. Lay flat with your BO tail on the right hand side.

SEW CO edge tog using the horizontal invisible seam stitch (page 117).

FILL your new pillowcase with a pillow insert, poly-fil or scrap yarn.

SEW BO edge tog. Weave ends in to inside.

# HOME

## MODERN KNITS FOR COZYING UP INDOORS

**WHEN CHRIS AND I MOVED** into our first apartment together, we wanted to make it a home by incorporating elements of our respective selves. I started knitting items for around the house that were not only decorative but durable and served a purpose.

All of the pieces in this chapter can be used on the daily. From rugs to ottomans, the Home chapter will feature stiff textures, durable knits and stylish accents that will make your home warm and cozy. A few of them feature machine washable yarns, such as Ember's Circle Rug (page 89) and Walter's Ottoman (page 101) while others are made with yarn that incorporates plastic and help our environment!

Whether for your home or a loved one's, these decorative home pieces will add a touch of warmth and lots of love to any space.

# EMBER'S CIRCLE RUG

This rug uses the mighty Tough Love by Love Fest Fibers. Not only is it tough and can withstand being stepped on, it's also machine washable! You can throw it in the dryer (air only) but I recommend laying it out flat to dry. As it's a circle, it makes a nice statement rug in the bathroom or by the kitchen sink. Using US 50 (25-mm) knitting needles, you'll start at the center of the circle and work your way outward. This is a fun technical piece that teaches you how to knit a flat circle and leads to everyday use.

## YARN

Love Fest Fibers Tough Love (25 ounces [709 g], 50 yards [46 m], 100% New Zealand wool):

- 5 balls, Oatmeal Stripe

## GAUGE

In stockinette st, 2¼ st and 3¼ rows = 4 inches (10 cm). To save time, take time to check gauge.

## FINISHED MEASUREMENTS

34-inch (86-cm) diameter

## NEEDLES

2 sets of US 50 (25-mm) 36-inch (91-cm) circular needles, or size needed to obtain correct gauge

## NOTIONS

Hair clip or scrap yarn to mark the beginning of the round

Use your fingers to weave in ends

## TECHNIQUES

Stockinette Stitch (page 123)

Join in the Round (page 119)

## DESIGNER NOTE

The fun thing about this rug is that either side can be the front! I myself like the backside up.

## NOW LET'S GET KNITTING!

USE 2 sets of circular needles for the entire project.

CO 8 sts. Join in the round, being careful not to twist the sts; pm.

RND 1: K.

RND 2: Incr every stitch by knitting twice into the same stitch (16 sts).

RND 3: K.

RND 4: *K1, yo; rep from * around (32 sts).

RNDS 5–7: K.

RND 8: *K2, yo; rep from * around (48 sts).

RNDS 9–10: K.

RND 11: *K3, YO; rep from * around (64 sts).

RNDS 12–13: K.

RND 14: *K4, YO; rep from * around (80 sts).

RND 15: K.

## FINISHING

BO. Weave in ends. Step all over your beautiful new rug!

# RHYTHM RUG

Designed for daily use, the Rhythm Rug works great out in front of your home or as you step out of the shower. Using 100 percent cotton rope from a female-run Portland-based company, Modern Macramé, the rug is machine washable! To dry, lay it out flat, placing heavy books on the corners to prevent curling.

## FIBER
Modern Macramé 5-mm Cotton Rope
(12 ounces [340 g], 33 yards [30 m],
100% cotton):

• 5 bundles Mint

## GAUGE
In stockinette st, 5 st and 6.6 rows = 4 inches
(10 cm). This pattern is not overly dependent
on gauge.

## FINISHED MEASUREMENTS
36 x 20 inches (91 x 51 cm)

## NEEDLES
US 35 (19-mm) 36-inch (91-cm) or longer circular
needles, or size needed to obtain correct gauge

## NOTIONS
Crochet hook to weave in ends

## TECHNIQUE
Stockinette Stitch (page 123)

## NOW LET'S GET KNITTING!
CO 43 sts.

NOTE. Slip sts at beg of each row pwise.

ROW 1 AND ALL ODD ROWS: Sl1, p across.

ROW 2: Sl1, k across.

ROW 4: Sl1, k3, yo, ssk, k31, k2tog, yo, k4.

ROW 6: Sl1, k across.

ROW 8: Sl1, k8, yo, ssk, k21, k2tog, yo, k9.

ROW 10: Sl1, k across.

ROW 12: Sl1, k13, yo, ssk, k11, k2tog, yo, k14.

ROW 14: Sl1, k across.

ROW 16: Sl1, k18, yo, ssk, k1, k2tog, yo, k to end.

NOTE: the slant of the decrease changes now.

ROW 18: Sl1, k18, yo, k2tog, k1, ssk, yo, k to end.

ROW 20: Sl1, k across.

ROW 22: Sl1, k13, yo, k2tog, k11, ssk, yo, k14.

ROW 24: Sl1, k across.

ROW 26: Sl1, k8, yo, k2tog, k21, ssk, yo, k9.

ROW 28: Sl1, k across.

ROW 30: Sl1, k3, yo, k2tog, k31, ssk, yo, k4.

ROW 32: Sl1, k across.

ROW 33: Sl1, p across.

## FINISHING
BO.

WEAVE IN all ends.

# BLACKSHEEP'S ARM KNIT BLANKET

If you read the introduction to this book, you'll know about BlackSheepMade, my fiber goods business where I knit unique items for you, your home and your pets, no two being the same! The name for this blanket is a spinoff of my brand, but also a testament to how unique each blanket is.

Arm knitting is perfect for both beginners and experienced knitters alike; this technique does not need any extra tools. Your forearms are your needles! The end result is both impressive and satisfying!

Now I will warn you, this blanket can be a bit of an arm workout! While it can most definitely be done in one sitting, you may want to set it down to give your arms a rest. Using your arms as the needles creates a net-like texture, but the yarn itself keeps your fabric loose but cozy.

## YARN
Woolly Mahoosive Giant Merino (2.2 pounds [1 kg], yardage varies, 19.5-micron superfine merino, roving style yarn):

- 1 ball Light Gray

## GAUGE
In stockinette st, 3 sts = 6 inches (15 cm) and 2 rows = 4 inches (10 cm). To save time, take time to check gauge.

## FINISHED MEASUREMENTS
40 x 60 inches (102 x 152 cm)

## NEEDLES
Your arms! Or US 50 (25-mm) straight needles, or size needed to obtain correct gauge

## NOTIONS
Your fingers! Or 50-mm crochet hook for weaving in ends

## TECHNIQUES
Stockinette Stitch (page 123)

Arm Knitting (page 109)

## NOW LET'S GET ARM KNITTING!
CO 16 sts.

ROW 1: K.

ROW 2: P.

ROWS 3–5: K.

REP rows 2–5 until your work measures 60 inches (152 cm). End on Row 2.

## FINISHING
BO. Weave in all ends.

# HOMEBODY BLANKET

I love a good road trip or outdoor adventure, but I also love my couch! I'm a bit of a homebody. This blanket is perfect for the winter months when you want to hibernate and keep away from the world. It's big enough to cover a full-size bed or cozy up on the couch. The woolly yarn will keep you warm but the design will keep the blanket from being too hot when in use.

It requires a closer eye due to the several yarn overs but is still a speedy knit thanks to the garter stitch sprinkled throughout. Be sure not to add extra unnecessary stitches by knitting the YOs throughout the pattern.

## YARN
Wool and the Gang Crazy Sexy Wool
(7 ounces [200 g], 87 yards [80 m], 100% wool):

- 10 balls Eucalyptus Green

## GAUGE
In garter st, 5 sts and 10 rows = 4 inches (10 cm). This pattern is not overly dependent on gauge.

## FINISHED MEASUREMENTS
54 x 67 inches (137 x 170 cm)

## NEEDLES
US 35 (19-mm) needles, or size needed to obtain correct gauge

## NOTIONS
Darning needle or crochet hook for weaving in ends

## TECHNIQUE
Garter Stitch (page 115)

## NOW LET'S GET KNITTING!
CO 66 sts.

ROWS 1-3: K across.

ROW 4: K6, *yo, k1, yo2, k1, yo3, k1, yo2, k1, yo, k6; rep from *.

ROW 5: K across, dropping all the yo's.

ROW 6: K1, *yo, k1, yo2, k1, yo3, k1, yo2, k1, yo, k6; rep from *, end with k1 instead of k6 on last repeat.

ROW 7: K across, dropping all the yo's.

ROWS 8-13: K every row (6 rows).

ROWS 14-17: Repeat rows 4-9.

ROWS 18-25: K every row (8 rows).

ROWS 26-29: Repeat rows 4-9.

ROWS 30-45: K every row (16 rows).

ROWS 46-49: Repeat rows 4-9.

ROWS 50-55: K every row (6 rows).

(CONTINUED)

**ROWS 56-59:** Repeat rows 4-9.

**ROWS 60-65:** K every row (6 rows).

**ROWS 66-69:** Repeat rows 4-9.

**ROWS 70-85:** K every row (16 rows).

**ROWS 86-89:** Repeat rows 4-9.

**ROWS 90-97:** K every row (8 rows).

**ROWS 98-101:** Repeat rows 4-9.

**ROWS 102-107:** K every row (6 rows).

**ROWS 108-111:** Repeat rows 4-9.

**ROWS 112-114:** K every row.

## FINISHING

BO. Weave in ends.

# YAMHILL BLANKET

A classic throw size, the Yamhill Blanket is sure to keep you and your guests warm. Knitting blankets can be a daunting task because of their size and time commitment. Although they feel like such a huge accomplishment, they take ages! Luckily with big yarn and big needles, this adventure flies by pretty quickly.

Featuring Love Fest Fibers' ReLove Alpaca in beautiful herringbone, this quick throw blanket is earth-friendly, saving fifteen plastic bottles per 100 yards (91 m) of yarn. Chunky yarn with a cause! When you feel the yarn, you'd never guess there is plastic spun with the alpaca or merino.

## YARN
Love Fest Fibers ReLove Alpaca (36 ounces [1020 g], 100 yards [91 m], ⅔ undyed alpaca fiber; ⅓ Global Recycle Standard Certified rPET; recycled cotton core):

- 3 bumps Dove Grey

## GAUGE
In herringbone st, 5¼ sts and 3½ rows = 4 inches (10 cm). This pattern is not overly dependent on gauge.

## FINISHED MEASUREMENTS
30 x 50 inches (76 x 127 cm)

## NEEDLES
US 50 (25-mm) circular needles, or size needed to obtain correct gauge

## NOTIONS
US 19 (15-mm) crochet hook for weaving in ends

## TECHNIQUES
Herringbone Stitch (page 117)

## NOW LET'S GET KNITTING!
CO 66 sts.

KNIT in herringbone stitch until your piece measures 30 inches (76 cm).

## FINISHING
BO tightly, as herringbone tends to widen out as you bind off. You want to ensure your top and bottom edges are the same width.

WEAVE IN all ends.

# WALTER'S OTTOMAN

Walter's Ottoman is another deep dive into furniture. Worked up in multiple colors of the beloved Tough Love yarn, it features the double moss stitch. I use scrap rope and yarn to fill it but you're welcome to use your choice of scraps, foam or poly-fil.

When I first began knitting, I really hadn't thought beyond scarves and beanies. I knew I eventually wanted to knit a sweater. And of course, a matching sweater for Winston, my dog. When I came across Love Fest Fibers, I was overjoyed with the idea that knits didn't have to be delicate. They could make tough, sturdy and structurally sound utilitarian pieces too!

Walter's Ottoman is constructed in six separate panels. After knitting the panels, you'll seam together the edges using a crochet hook, giving it a nice finished edge. Tough Love has a wide range of colors, from neutrals to bright pops and even self-striping! You can really make each ottoman unique.

## YARN
Love Fest Fibers Tough Love (25 ounces [709 g], 50 yards [46 m], 100% New Zealand wool):

- 2 balls Teal (Color A)
- 2 balls Oatmeal Stripe (Color B)
- 2 balls Heather Grey (Color C )

## GAUGE
In double moss st, 2.75 sts and 4 rows = 4 inches (10 cm). This pattern is not overly dependent on gauge.

## FINISHED MEASUREMENTS
20-inch (51-cm) cube

## NEEDLES
US size 50 (25-mm) straight needles, or size needed to obtain correct gauge

## NOTIONS
Crochet hook for seaming and weaving in ends

Scrap yarn, rope foam or poly-fil, for stuffing

## TECHNIQUES
Double Moss Stitch (page 115)

Slip Stitch (crochet) (page 123)

## NOW LET'S GET KNITTING!

### PANELS 1 AND 2
WITH COLOR A, CO 14 sts.

WORK in double moss st until your piece measures 20 inches (51 cm).

BO and set aside.

### PANELS 3 AND 4
WITH COLOR B, CO 14 sts.

WORK in double moss st until your piece measures 20 inches (51 cm).

BO and set aside.

### PANELS 5 AND 6
WITH COLOR C, CO 14 sts.

WORK in double moss st until your piece measures 20 inches (51 cm).

BO and set aside.

HOME

(CONTINUED)

## FINISHING

PLACE your panels side by side in whichever order you desire.

SEAM the edges tog using a crochet hook: Take 40 inches (102 cm) of Tough Love and panels 1 and 3, holding them with their WS touching. Make a slip knot and place it onto the crochet hook. Beg at the RH side of the edge to be seamed, insert hook from front to back through both pieces. YO and bring the yarn back through both pieces of yarn and through the loop on your hook. Rep this process until you've gone across the entire edge. Check out the slip stitch crochet technique on page 123.

NOW grab your next panel and join it in the same manner. Continue to do this until you have 1 panel left.

BEFORE you close up your ottoman and join the last panel, you'll want to fill it up! Grab scrap yarn or rope or your favorite poly-fil. Fill it up as much as you desire. I myself like a very stiff ottoman so I packed mine!

JOIN your last panel to the rest of the cube.

If you have any ends sticking out, such as cast-on or cast-off tails, just stuff them inside the ottoman at the corners.

# STITCH ABBREVIATIONS

BEG - beginning

BO - bind off

BOR - beginning of round

BRK - brioche knit. Knit the next st with its yo.

BRP - brioche purl. Purl the next st with its yo.

CO - cast on

DECR - decrease

DPN - double pointed needles

EOR - end of round

HBS - half brioche stitch

INCR - increase

K/K - knit

KWISE - knitwise, as if to knit

K2TOG - knit 2 together

K1TBL - knit 1 through the back loop

LA - left arm

LH - left hand

M1L - make 1 left. Make 1 stitch by picking up the stitch below the stitch on the LH needle and knitting it through the back loop.

P/P - purl

P1TBL - purl 1 through the back loop

P2TOG - purl two together

P2TOGTBL - purl two together through the back loop

PM - place marker

PREV - previous

PWISE - purl wise, as if to purl

REM - remaining

REP - repeat

RA - right arm

RH - right hand

RM - remove marker

RND - round

RS - right side

SL - slip

(CONTINUED)

**SL1YO** - slip the next stitch purlwise, then bring the yarn over the needle and across the slipped stitch to the back of the needle

**SL1WYIF** - bring the yarn to the front between your needles. Slip 1 st p-wise then bring the yarn to the back between your needles.

**SM** - slip marker

**SSK** – slip, slip, knit. Slip the first stitch on your LH needle to your RH needle knitwise. Repeat with the second stitch. Now knit both stitches together by slipping your LH needle through the stitches and in front of your RH needle.

**ST/STS** – stitch/stitches

**TOG** - together

**T2B** - twist two back. After working to the position of the twist, k into the second st on the LH needle, being careful not to drop the original st and leaving the st on the LH needle. Pm. Bring the yarn to the front of the work and p the first stitch on the LH needle. Slide both sts off the LH needle. You now have your 2 new twisted sts on the RH needle with a marker in between them. The knit st will slant to the right and sit on top of the purled st.

**WS** – wrong side

**YB** - bring yarn to back of work between the needles

**YFWD** - bring yarn to front of work between the needles

**YO** - yarn over

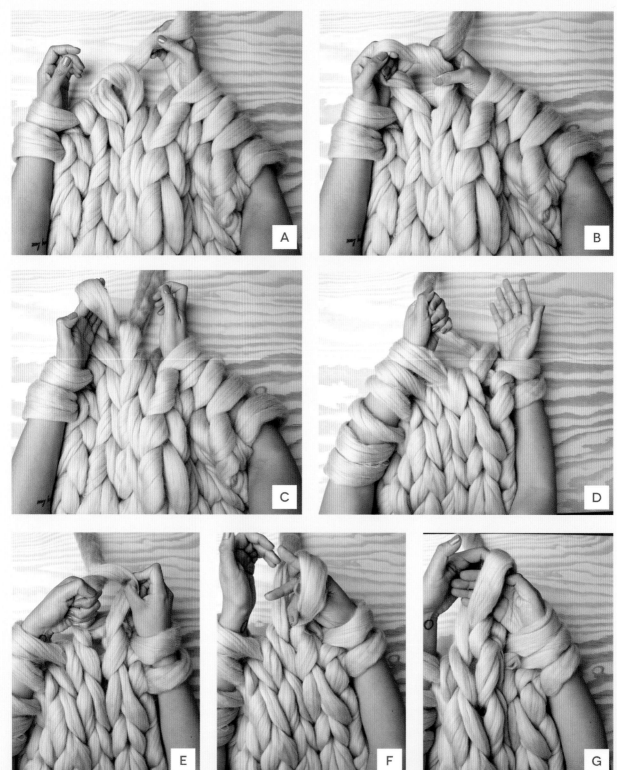

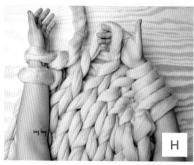
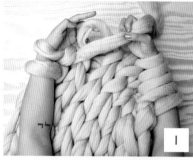

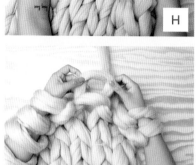

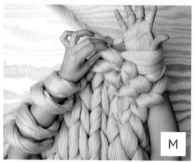

# TECHNIQUES

## ARM KNITTING

Just like regular old knitting—but with your arms and ginormous yarn. With arm knitting, you'll make a slip knot for your cast on (page 113) just as you normally would if you were using needles. Same goes for the actual casting on. Here I will abbreviate right arm/hand as RA/H and left arm/hand as LA/H.

TO CAST ONTO YOUR ARMS: Pull 3 wingspans (roughly 15' [4.5 m]) of yarn and make a slip knot. Slip the loop onto your right arm/hand. Similar to the Cast On technique on page 113, place the working yarn between your middle and pointer fingers. Wrap the tail around your thumb. Slip your right hand under your thumb, creating a loop with the yarn. Then pull the working yarn through that loop and onto your right hand/arm. Repeat this step until you have reached the desired number of stitches.

TO KNIT (RIGHT ARM TO LEFT ARM) (SEE LEFT PAGE TOP TWO ROWS): Slip the first stitch onto your LA. Take the next stitch off of your RA then grab the working yarn in your RH (A). Using your LH, pull the yarn through the stitch you just took off (B) and place the new stitch on your LA (C). Repeat this until the end of your row.

TO KNIT (LEFT ARM TO RIGHT ARM) (SEE LEFT PAGE TOP BOTTOM ROW): Slip the first stitch onto your RA. With your LH grab the working yarn (D), pulling it through the first stitch from back to front on your LA (E). Slip this new stitch onto your RH (F-G). Repeat this until the end of your row.

TO PURL (RIGHT ARM TO LEFT ARM) (SEE ABOVE TOP ROW): Slip the first stitch onto your LA. Take the next stitch off your RH (H), placing it behind the working yarn (I). Pull the yarn through the stitch from front to back (J), placing the new stitch on your LA. Repeat this until the end of your row.

TO PURL (LEFT ARM TO RIGHT ARM) (SEE ABOVE BOTTOM ROW): Slip the first stitch onto your RA. Take the next stitch off your LH (K), placing it behind the working yarn. Pull the yarn through the stitch from front to back (L), placing the new stitch on your RA (M). Repeat this until the end of your row.

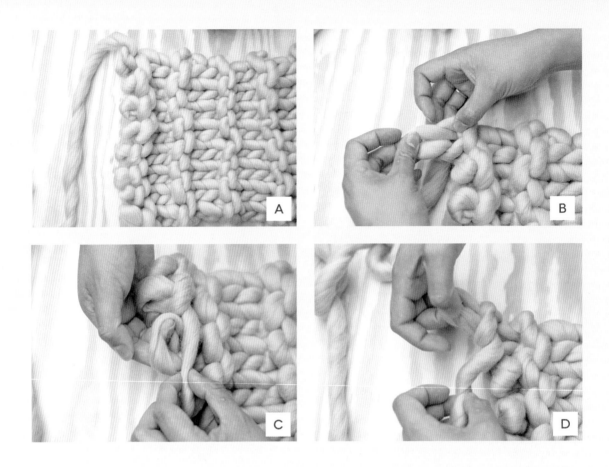

## ARM KNITTING—ALTERNATE TECHNIQUE

In this technique, used for the Chelsea Arm Knit Cowl (page 52), lay your work flat on a table.

CREATE A SLIP KNOT. With your fingers, pull a 2-inch (5-cm) loop through the slip knot, from back to front. For the next stitch, pull another 2-inch (5-cm) loop through the new stitch you just made. Repeat until you have your desired number of stitches.

TO KNIT: Lay your chain of stitches out flat. The working yarn should be on the right side of your work. Place it above your chain. Pull the yarn through the last loop (A), as if you were chaining another stitch, creating a new 2-inch (5-cm) loop (B).

MOVE one stitch over to the left and pull the yarn through that stitch from back to front, creating another 2-inch (5-cm) loop. Repeat, moving one stitch to the left, until you've reached the end of the row.

Your working yarn should now be on the left of your work. Lay it above this new row of stitches. To continue knitting, repeat the step above.

TO PURL: Instead of laying your working yarn above your previous row, lay it on top. Take your fingers and pull the working yarn through the previous stitch from front to back (C), creating a 2-inch (5-cm) loop (D).

MOVE one stitch to the right. From front to back, pull a 2-inch (5-cm) loop. Repeat to the end of your row.

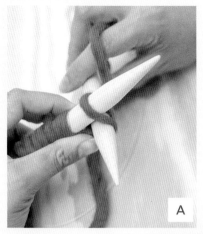

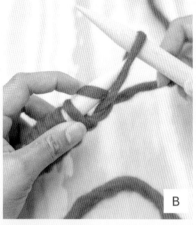

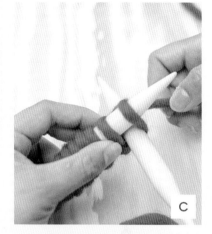

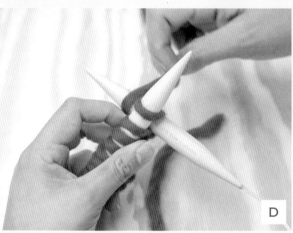

## ALTERNATE RIB CAST ON

The alternate rib cast on allows for a cleaner edge when creating a piece that starts out in a rib pattern. You'll alternate between a knit cast on and a purl cast on.

START WITH A SLIP KNOT. Knit the slip knot, placing the new stitch on the needle.

STEP ONE: Insert your right needle in between the two stitches from back to front (A). With your working yarn in front, purl and place the new stitch on your needle (B).

STEP TWO: Insert your right needle in between the two stitches from front to back (C). Knit and place the new stitch on your needle (D).

ALTERNATE these two steps until you've reached your desired number of stitches.

## BASKETWEAVE PATTERN (SEE BOTTOM RIGHT PHOTO)

Worked in the round on a multiple of 10 sts, 10 row rep.

RNDS 1-5: *K5, p5; rep from * to end of rnd.

RNDS 6-10: *P5, k5; rep from * to end of rnd.

REP rnds 1-10, as directed in pattern.

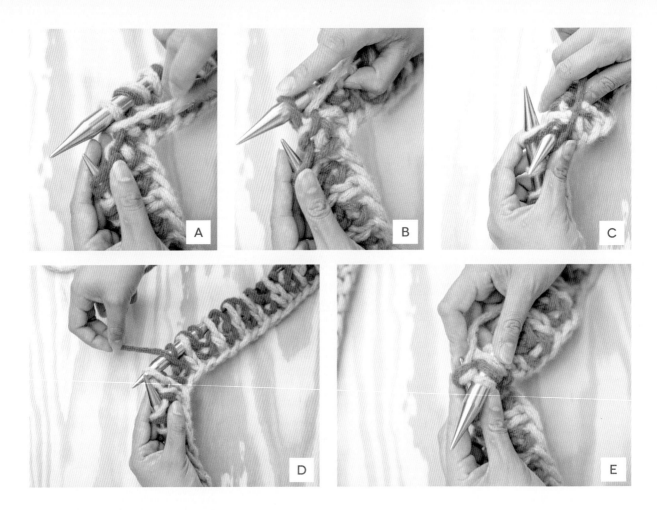

## BRIOCHE

Brioche knitting can feel a bit involved but has a worthy end result. Use this technique for patterns in this book such as the Morrison Cowl (page 51).

RND 1 (SET-UP ROUND): With Color A, *yfwd, sl1yo, k1; rep from * around (A-B).

RND 2: With Color B, *BRP, sl1yo; rep from * around (C-D).

RND 3: With Color A, *yfwd, sl1yo, BRK; rep from * around (E).

REP rnds 2 and 3 ten times. You will be alternating colors each round (Color A for odd rounds and Color B for even rounds). You should end with Color B.

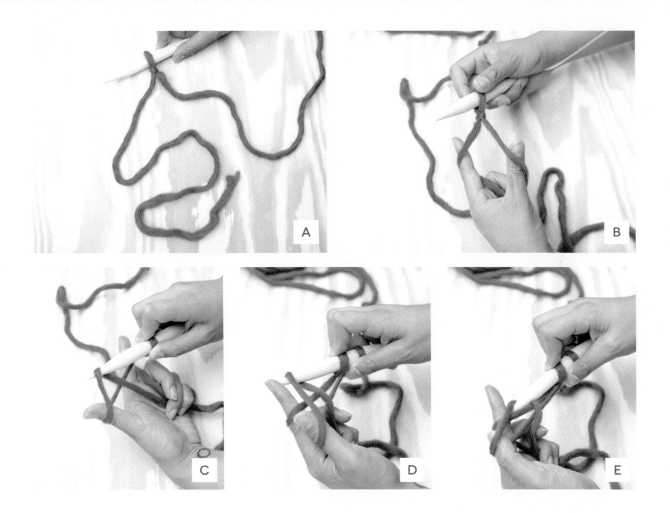

## CAST ON

For most of the patterns in this book I use the longtail cast-on method, unless otherwise stated. Here's how to do it:

MAKE A SLIP KNOT, leaving a long tail. The more stitches, the longer the tail needed.

PLACE the slip knot on your right needle, the working yarn (yarn that is attached to ball) in the back and the tail in front (A).

SLIP your left thumb and index finger in between the two strands and wrap your last three fingers around both strands of yarn (B).

WHILE holding your left hand in the shape of an L (palm facing you), pick up the strand wrapped around your thumb, creating a loop (C).

NOW, bring the yarn wrapped around your index finger through that loop (D–E). Drop the loop on your thumb and pull to tighten new stitch. Repeat these steps until your desired number of stitches is achieved.

TECHNIQUES

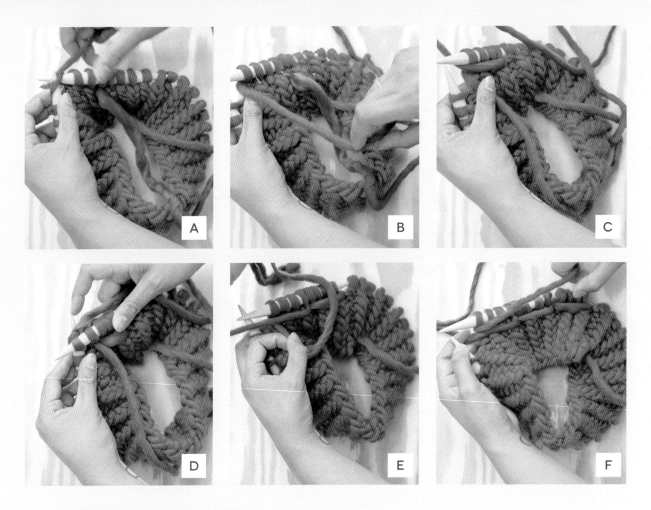

## COLORFUL LINEN STITCH

A twist on the traditional linen stitch and Fair Isle knitting, where instead of carrying the non-working yarn behind your work, you'll carry it in front of your work.

WITH COLOR A ready to knit at the back of the work, attach Color B and bring it to the front of the work, leaving Color A behind the work. K4 using Color A (A).

SWITCH COLORS by bringing Color A to the front of your work (B) and Color B across the front of your work and to the back (C). K4 in color B (D).

SWITCH COLORS again by bringing Color A across the front of your work and to the back (E); now you'll bring Color B to the front. k4 in Color A (F).

CONTINUE to repeat, switching colors all the way around.

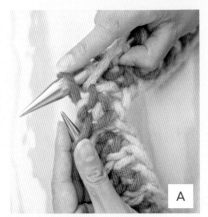

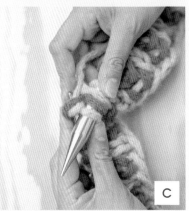

## DOUBLE MOSS STITCH (PHOTO TOP LEFT)

Worked on a multiple of 2 sts, 4 row rep.

ROW 1: *K1, p1; rep from * across.

ROW 2: *P1, k1; rep from * across.

ROW 3: *P1, k1; rep from * across.

ROW 4: *K1, p1; rep from * across.

REP rows 1–4 for pattern.

## GARTER STITCH (WORKED FLAT) (PHOTO TOP RIGHT)

Knit every stitch on every row.

## HALF BRIOCHE STITCH

Just like the brioche stitch, except we are only working one of the rows.

SET UP: yfwd, sl1 pwise, yo, k1. Repeat this until the end of your row (A).

ROW 1 (BRK): knit the stitches with their paired yo's (B–C).

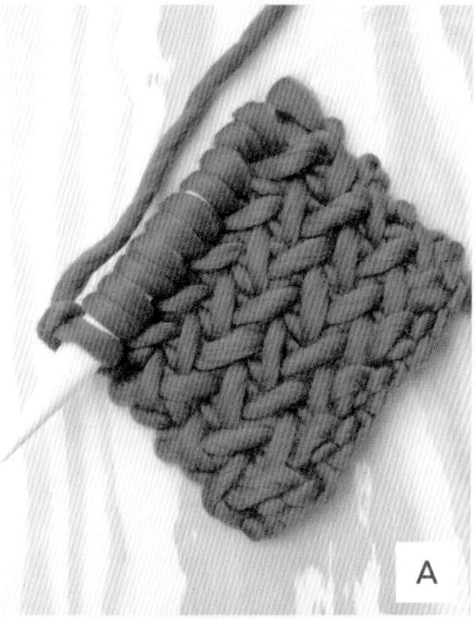
A

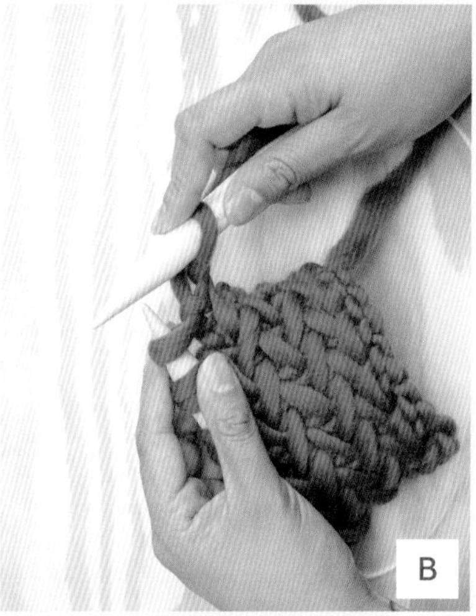
B

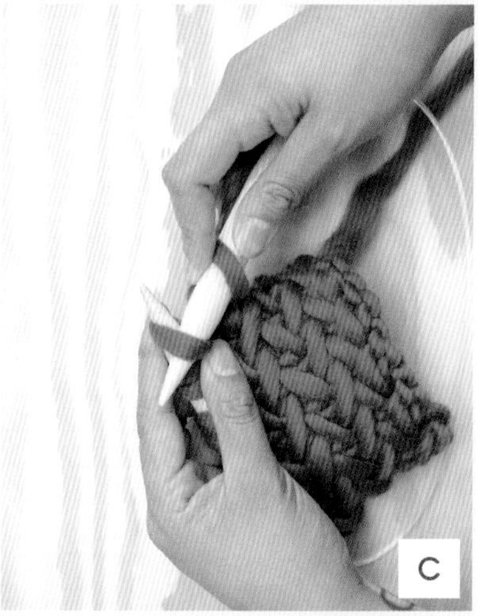
C

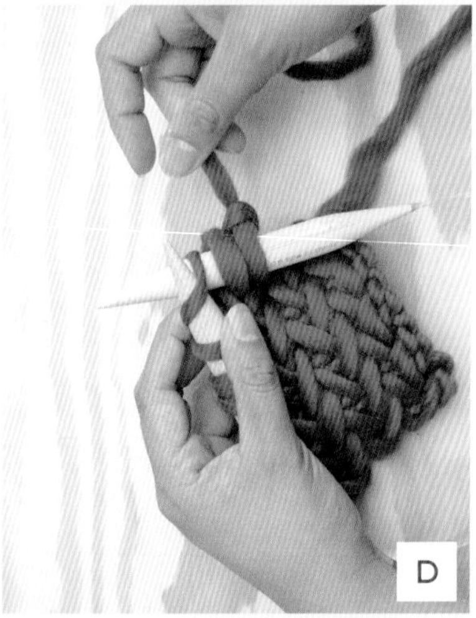
D

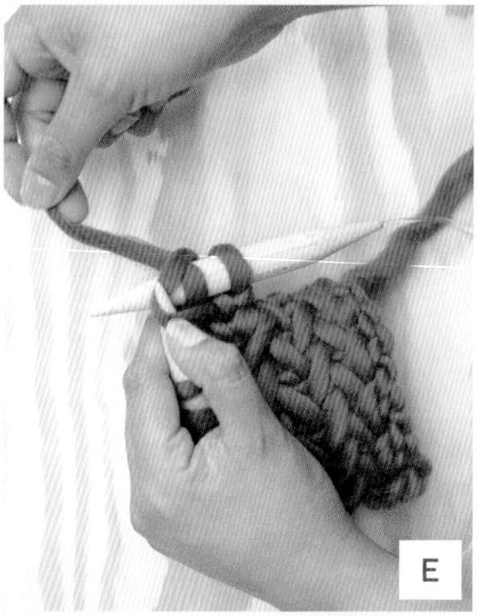
E

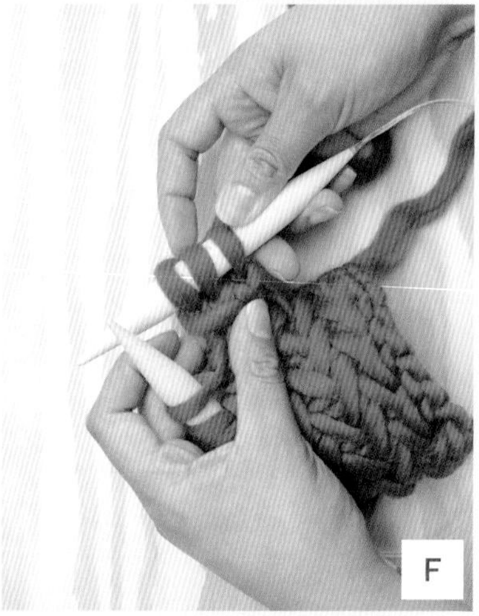
F

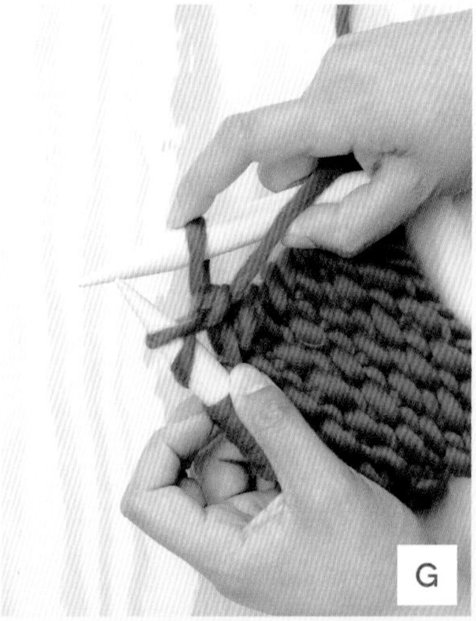
G

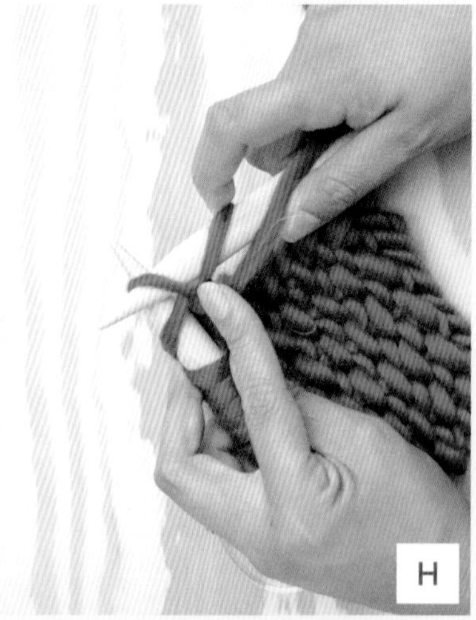
H

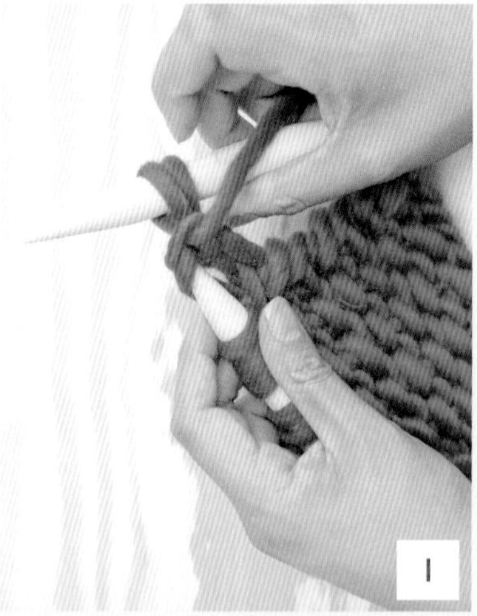
I

## HERRINGBONE STITCH (PHOTOS TO THE LEFT)

Herringbone has a zig-zag look to it and creates a firm fabric (A).

ROW 1 (RS): K1 (B), *sl1 kwise (C), k1 (D); with LH needle, lift slipped stitch over, but do not drop it off the LH needle, k the slipped st (E–F); rep from * across, ending k1.

ROW 2 (WS): P2tog but don't drop from needle (G), p into first st on LH needle again (H), sl both sts off LH needle (I).

REP these 2 rows to create the pattern.

## HORIZONTAL INVISIBLE SEAM STITCH (PHOTO ABOVE)

A great seaming technique when you're looking for a clean, invisible finish.

LINE UP your bind-off and cast-on edges so the stitches in each row line up with one another. Take a length of yarn and thread it thorough your darning needle. Slip the needle into the bottom right corner of your top piece.

BRING the yarn through the corresponding corner (top right) of your bottom piece to connect the two edges.

THREAD YOUR DARNING NEEDLE under both legs of the first V of the top piece and pull the yarn through. Now thread your darning needle under the corresponding V stitch on the bottom piece side and pull the yarn through.

MOVING ONE STITCH TO THE LEFT, thread your darning needle under the corresponding V stitch, threading through the same gap your first stitch came out. Continue to move between your two edges, slipping your needle through.

PULL RIGHT to bring the edges together.

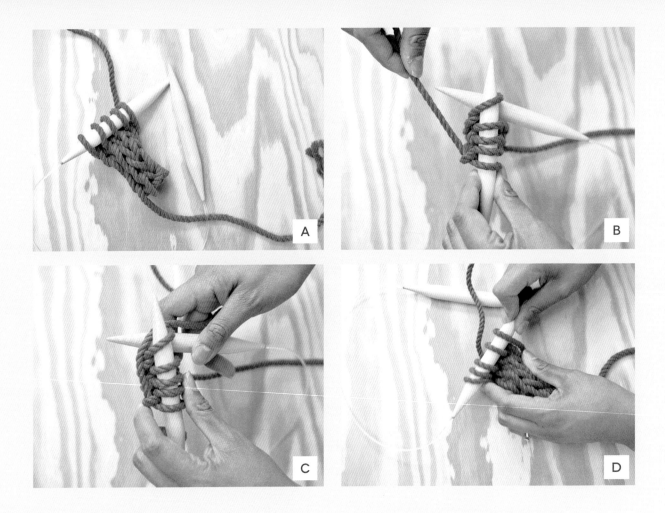

## I-CORD

A knitted cord that is great for bag handles, hat toppers or a Tug-o-War Toy (page 79)!

USING either DPNs or circular needles, cast on your desired number of stitches (A).

SLIDE YOUR STITCHES to the other end of the needle. Your working yarn will be on the left side of the stitches.

KNIT your first stitch, pulling the working yarn across the back of your work (B). After you knit the first stitch, pull snug to ensure you've closed the gap. Knit until the end of your row (C).

SLIDE YOUR STITCHES to the other end of your needles and repeat this process until your I-cord has reached your desired length (D).

## INTARSIA (PHOTOS ON NEXT PAGE)

Intarsia allows for big blocks of color while providing a tidy "wrong side" of the work. It also lessens the number of ends you have to weave in at the end.

RS: Work up to the point of the color change (B). Cross your current color over your new color (C). Bring the new color down into the knit position (D) and knit (E).

WS: Work up to the point of the color change (F). Bring your current color to purl position in front of your work, making sure it crosses over the new yarn. Bring your new color to the back (G) and knit (H).

## JOIN IN THE ROUND (PHOTO ABOVE)

There are plenty of ways to join in the round. This is just my preferred method.

ALIGN YOUR STITCHES so they sit in the round. Make sure the stitches aren't twisted.

TAKE THE FIRST STITCH on the LH needle and slip it to the RH needle. K the now first stitch on the LH needle. Place BOR marker.

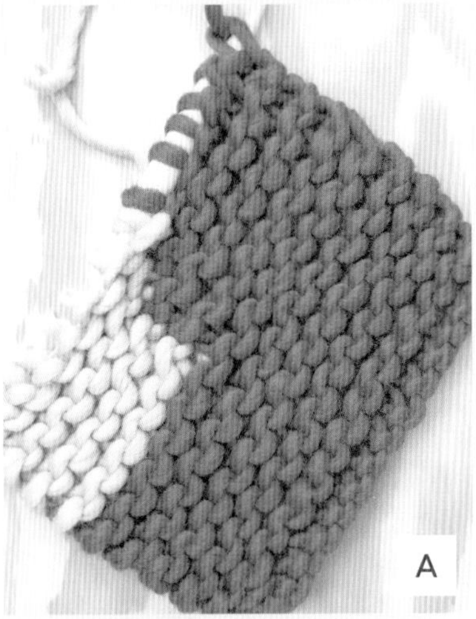
A
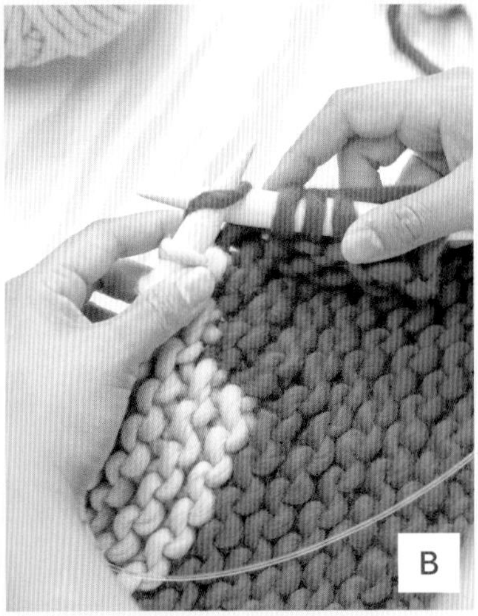
B
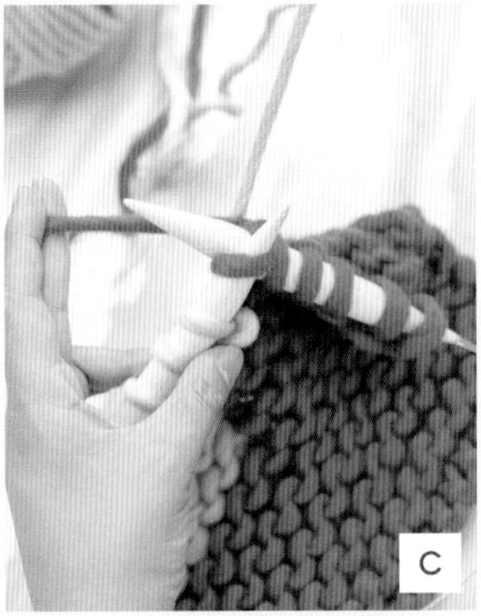
C
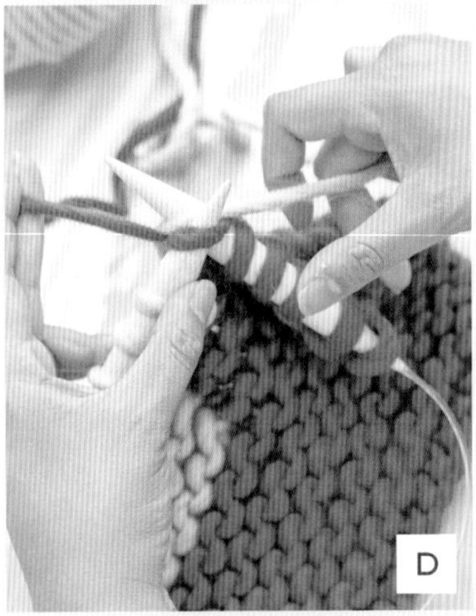
D
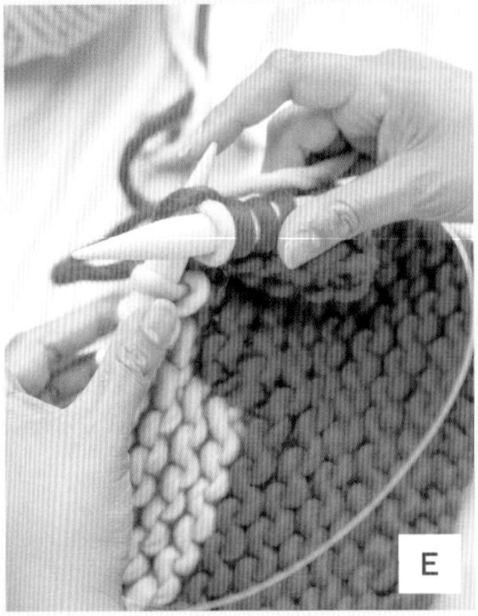
E
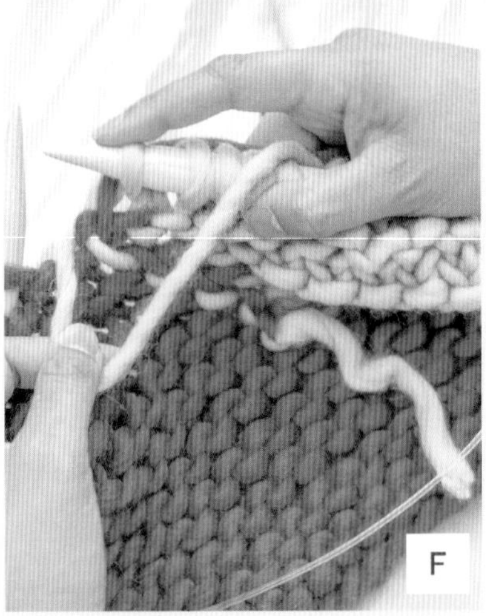
F
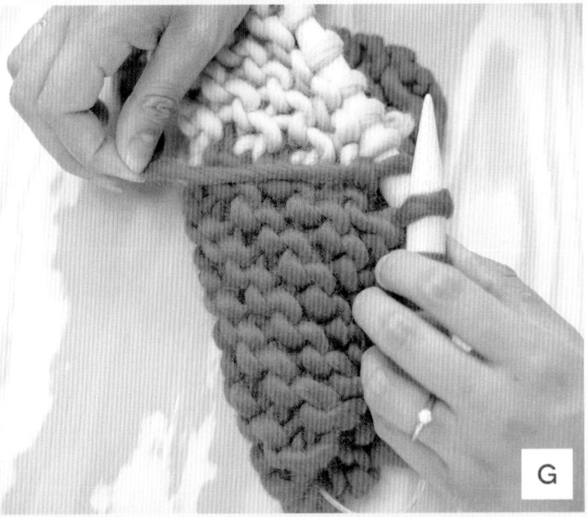
G
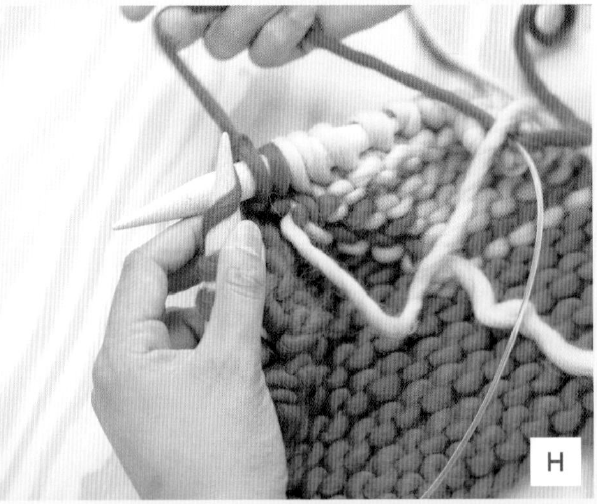
H

## LOOP STITCH (PHOTOS ON NEXT PAGE)

A fun way to add texture to any piece.

KNIT the stitch where you would like to add a loop, but do not remove the stitch from the needle (B).

BRING the yarn from the back to the front between the two needles (C). Form a loop around your thumb and bring the yarn to the back between the needles (D). Adjust the length of the loop and k the st on the LH needle (E). You have actually placed 2 sts on the RH needle at this point. Pass the first st over the second st on the RH needle and off (F–G). One loop completed.

## MISTAKE RIB (PHOTO ABOVE)

Worked in the round on a multiple of 4 sts, 2 rnd rep.

RND 1: *P2, k2; rep from * around.

RND 2: K1, *p2, k2; rep from * around, ending rnd with p2, k1.

REPEAT rnds 1 and 2 for pattern.

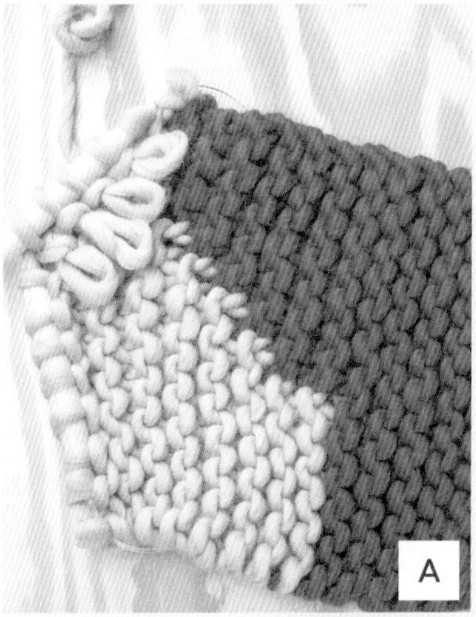
A
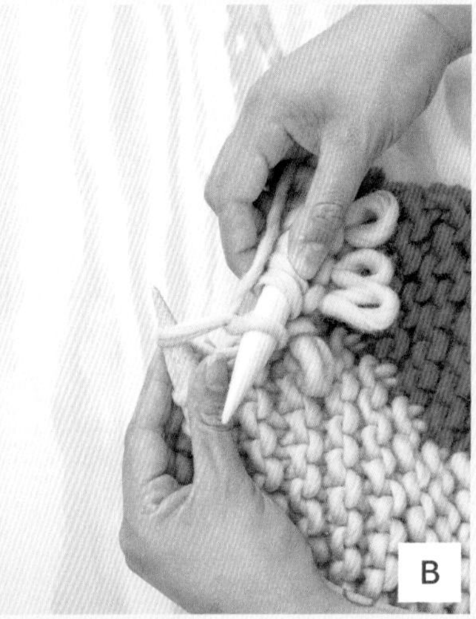
B
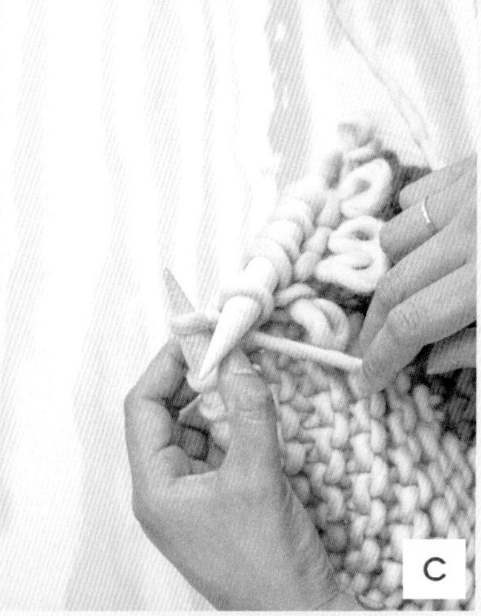
C
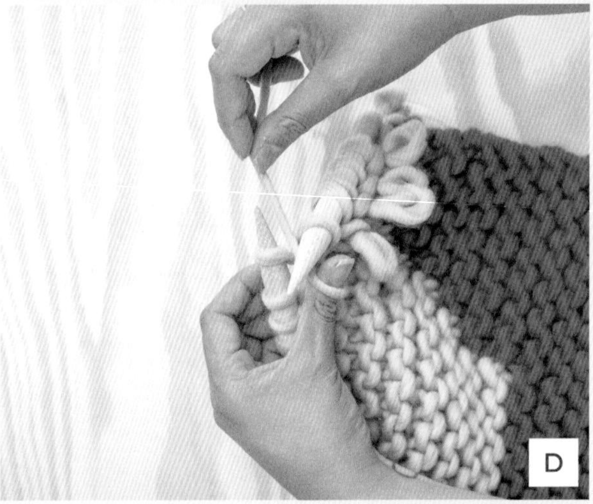
D
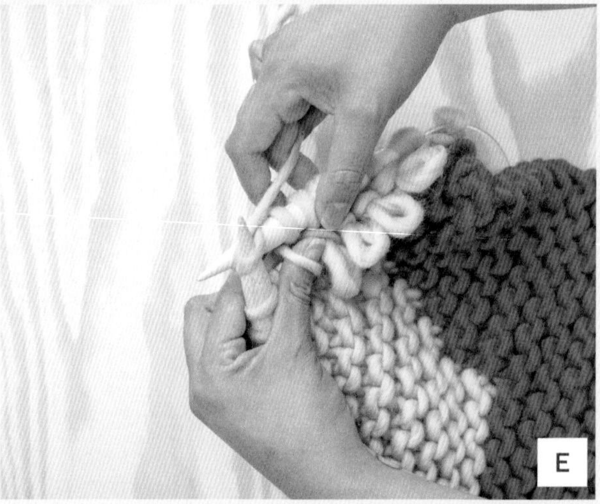
E
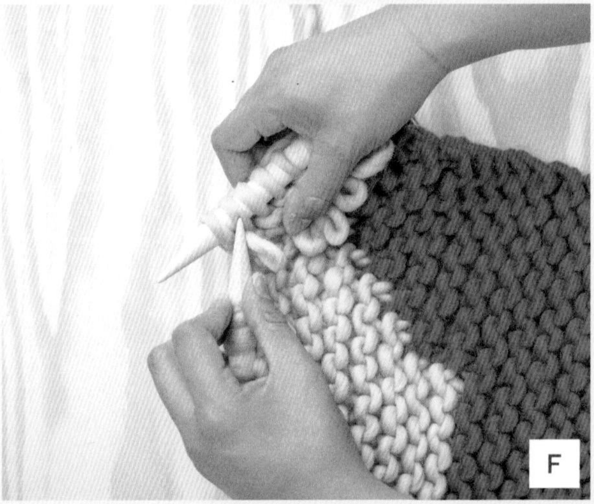
F
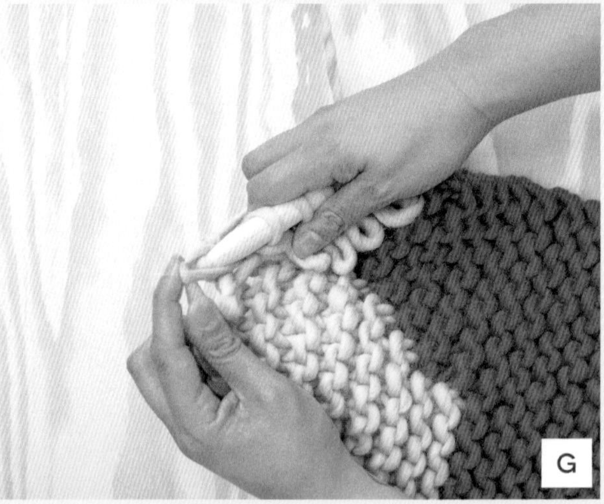
G

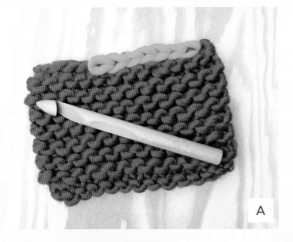
A

B

C

D

E

## SLIP STITCH (CROCHET) (PHOTOS ABOVE)

MAKE A SLIP KNOT and place it onto the crochet hook (B). Beg at the RH side of the edge to be seamed, insert hook from front to back through both pieces (C). Yo and bring the yarn back through both pieces of yarn and through the loop on your hook (D-E). Rep this process until you've gone across the entire edge.

## STOCKINETTE STITCH (WORKED FLAT) (PHOTO TO LEFT)

ON THE RS, knit every stitch. On the WS, purl every stitch.

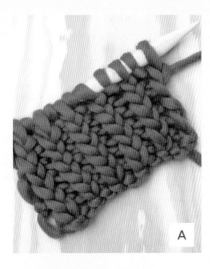  

## TWISTED RIB (PHOTOS ABOVE)

For a more defined yet stretchy rib, I like to knit and purl stitches through the back loop (k1tbl). It twists your stitches and adds more definition.

RND 1: *K1tbl (B), p1tbl (C); rep from * around.

REP Rnd 1 for pattern.

## 3-NEEDLE BIND OFF (PHOTOS RIGHT)

In order for your seam to be on the wrong side of your work, arrange your two pieces so the right sides are touching and the wrong side is facing outward (A). Hold your needles parallel to one another so the stitches line up. With a third needle of the same size (B–C), *knit the first stitch on each needle together. Drop both stitches off of their needles. You'll now have one stitch on your third needle. Now knit the new first two stitches on your original needles, as you did before, giving you two stitches on your third needle (D–E).

Using one of your original needles, slip the first stitch on your third needle over the second stitch and off the needle, as you would for your typical bind off (F–H). Repeat from * until you have one stitch left. Cut your yarn and pull it through the last stitch.

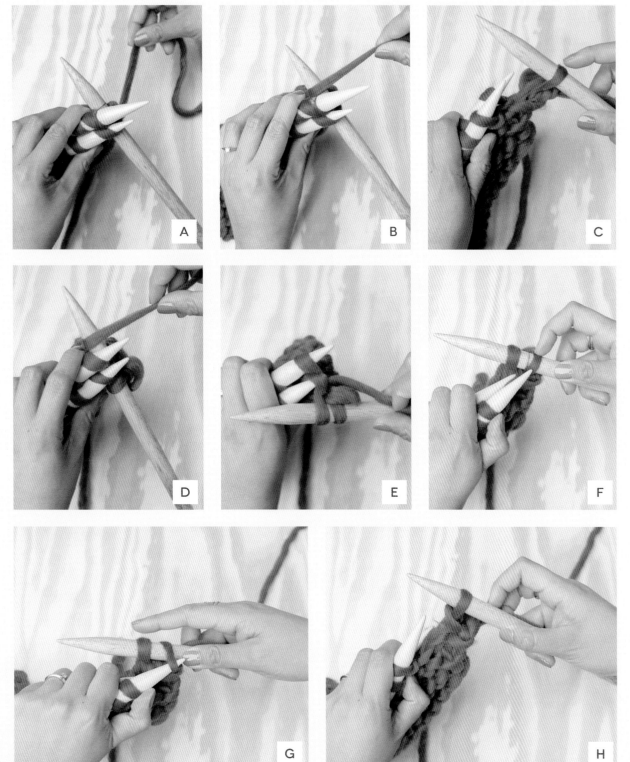

# YARN

Each pattern in this book is designed to use the yarn that is paired with the pattern. You can find all of these yarns online or at your LYS, local yarn store. Here is a list of those yarns plus others that can be used as substitutions.

## BROOKLYN TWEED, QUARRY, BROOKLYNTWEED.COM

This yarn can be used for Don's Night Cap (page 74) and Miss Van's Balaclava (page 70). If you substitute a different yarn the important thing is sticking to a bulky weight category. While the textures between yarn will vary, the main importance is to match the weight and gauge when substituting yarns.

SUBSTITUTION SUGGESTIONS: Nutmeg Fiber Arts Hearth, Sugarbush Dawson, Lion Brand Lion's Pride Woolspun.

## LOVE FEST FIBERS, TOUGH LOVE, LOVEFESTFIBERS.COM

Tough Love is used throughout the Home section (page 86) of this book. You may have a tough time finding a yarn like Tough Love. Love Fest Fibers created such a unique felted wool that there aren't many out there quite like it!

SUBSTITUTION SUGGESTIONS: Niroma Studio's Main Squeeze Wool or 8–10-mm soft braided cotton rope, Loopy Mango Tough Loop Merino Wool.

## MODERN MACRAMÉ, COTTON ROPE, MODERNMACRAME.COM

A few patterns in this book, such as the Rhythm Rug (page 90) and Tug-o-War Toy (page 79), require rope instead of yarn. This is a 3-ply rope and has a 5-mm thickness. Substituted ropes should be similar.

SUBSTITUTION SUGGESTION: Ganxxet Cotton Rope.

## LION BRAND, WOOL–EASE THICK AND QUICK, LIONBRAND.COM

Used for the Jax Scarf (page 80).

SUBSTITUTION SUGGESTIONS: Plymouth, Encore Mega Colorspun, Loops & Threads Cozy Wool.

(CONTINUED)

## LOVE FEST FIBERS, RELOVE ALPACA, LOVEFESTFIBERS.COM

Another unique yarn by Love Fest Fibers. There isn't another yarn quite like it either!

SUBSTITUTION SUGGESTIONS: Love Fest Fibers ReLove Merino, Loopy Mango Big Loop Yarn Merino Wool

## PLYMOUTH, VIENTO, PLYMOUTHYARN.COM

A bulky but airy yarn, Viento is used in Cada Día Beanie (page 69). If you substitute a different yarn, the important thing is sticking to a bulky weight category.

SUBSTITUTION SUGGESTIONS: Lion Brand Lion's Pride Woolspun, Sugarbush Dawson, Brooklyn Tweed Quarry.

## SUGARBUSH FARMS, DAWSON, SUGARBUSHFARMS.COM

Another light and airy yarn that still falls in the bulky category, Dawson is used in Miss Van's Balaclava (page 70). While the textures between yarn will vary, the main importance is to match the weight and gauge when substituting yarns.

## WOOL AND THE GANG, CRAZY SEXY WOOL, WOOLANDTHEGANG.COM

This yarn is used in the Scarves (page 12), Cowls (page 40) and Beanies (page 58) chapters. If you substitute a different yarn, the important thing is sticking to a super bulky weight category.

SUBSTITUTION SUGGESTIONS: We Are Knitters The Wool, Sugarbush Chill or Lion Brand Fifty Fifty.

## WOOLFOLK, HYGGE, WOOLFOLKYARN.COM

This is a chunky, chain-like yarn used in the Morrison Cowl (page 51) and can be used in the Radius Hooded Cowl (page 55). Due to Hygge's unusual construction, not many alternative yarns will give the exact same effect. If you substitute a different yarn, the important thing is sticking to a super bulky weight category. Loopy Mango's Big Cotton is soft, textured and has a similar gauge.

SUBSTITUTION SUGGESTIONS: Big Cotton or Loopy Mango Merino No. 5, We Are Knitters The Wool or Lion Brand Fifty Fifty.

## WOOLLY MAHOOSIVE, SQUIGGLY, WOOLLYMAHOOSIVE.COM

As this yarn is so unique, there are not many alternatives. If you want to use a different yarn, your best bet is searching Etsy for "chunky merino wool." You might even want to tack on "arm knitting" to that. You'll find a large variety of colors and weights.

SUBSTITUTION SUGGESTIONS: BettaKnit Big Hero Wool, Ohhio Helix, Love Fest Fibers ReLove Merino and/or Alpaca.

# ACKNOWLEDGMENTS

This book was an incredible triumph and it wouldn't have come together without these people:

I never thought a book was a goal of mine until the opportunity was presented to me by Page Street Publishing. Thanks to Rebecca Fofonoff and the Page Street team for seeking me out and believing in my work. For their patience and most of all for guiding me through this unfamiliar process.

Thanks to Dawn Seymore for her attention to detail during the technical editing phase and her endless support. I could not have done it without her expertise, her endless bowls of nuts and chocolates, or her yarn shop Fiber Rhythm Craft & Design where I spent many hours poring over the book and deciding which supplies to use. Dawn, these patterns would not have been presentable without your help.

To Kenny Hamlett, my photographer who has a natural eye for composition and lighting. It was a blast to share this project with you and navigate the world of being published together. Here's to all the late nights and back-to-back days spent going from business partners to friends. Working with a like-minded creative who was down for the hustle has been both inspiring and energizing.

To Stephanie Ibarra, Malia Jenkins and Lynsey Christensen for giving their time and energy to not only model my pieces but to be an ear when I needed it, for words of encouragement, and simply being badass babes I am fortunate to call my friends. Rock, thanks for staying up late and writing a handful of sentences peppered throughout this book. Malia, the best unofficial PA I will ever have, you think of every detail on and off the camera. Lynsey, without your morning texts full of encouragement, I would not have had the confidence to tackle this book day after day and of course for introducing me to Kenny.

Chris and Tyler thanks for showing that warm woolly knits can be unisex and taking time out of your schedules to be part of this.

I appreciate the generosity and kindness of the folks at Woolfolk, Love Fest Fibers and Starlight Knitting Society.

To my test knittas: you know who you are! I can't thank you all enough for knitting my patterns to life.

To Carol Lee, my business advisor from APANO. Carol you forced me to stop treating my business as a hobby and gave me access to resources that have helped me grow both as a person and a business.

A Mariela Bao for being my beginner knitter, talking me out of Imposter Syndrome, and giving me a taste of Latinx life in Portland.

The biggest hugs to my parents, for always encouraging me to forge my own path even when it was unconventional. Mom, you inspire me every day to be strong and face problems head on. Dad, I can't share my story and growth as an artist without mentioning you 1,000 times and for that I am grateful.

Extra belly rubs to Winston, Walter and Ember who cannot read as they are my dogs but were the cutest models, test subjects (for measuring) and fluffy pillows when I needed a break.

And last but absolutely not least, to my partner and best friend Christopher. Your unwavering support for me and my aspirations is something I will never be able to thank you for enough. You make my website look sleek, remind me not to forget the business side of running a business and keep the house clean 25/8. No matters.

# ABOUT THE AUTHOR

Alyssarhaye Graciano is a trilingual, POC fiber artist. Once in the tech industry as a linguistic specialist, she left her day job to pursue a creative career. While she mainly knits; crochet, macramé and weaving are also part of her everyday life.

She started BlackSheepMade as a way to fund an internship abroad while in college, but over the last three years it has evolved into large public installations, long-term pop-ups and traveling workshops. You can find her latest mural in her hometown of San Jose, California, at The Berryessa Flea. She wove a 15 x 8–foot (4.5x 2.5–m) mural with her dad, Francisco, as an homage to her late abuelita and hometown culture.

In 2018, she ran a two-month long pop-up in downtown Portland via a city-funded program. She was able to test out her idea of a "deli for knits": choose a style of beanie or scarf, pick your colors and she'll knit it up in a week.

Today, she continues her art career as a designer through Black Sheep Made and other various fiber brands and local businesses. She teaches fiber workshops near and far in both English and Spanish, her most recent one being in Tokyo, Japan, in October 2019.

Alyssarhaye lives in Portland, Oregon, with her partner Chris and their dogs Winston, Walter and Ember.

# INDEX

## A

alternating ribbing cast on

Cada Día Beanie, 69

Cascades Cowl, 44

technique, 111

arm knitting

Blacksheep's Arm Knit Blanket, 93

Chelsea Arm Knit Cowl, 52

Hella Big Arm Knit Scarf, 32

technique, 108–110

## B

Balaclava, Miss Van's, 70–73

basketweave pattern

Rhaye Cowl, 43

technique, 111

beanies, 59

Cada Día Beanie, 69

Multnomah Beanie, 61–62

PNW Beanie, 65–66

Blacksheep's Arm Knit Blanket, 93

blankets

Blacksheep's Arm Knit Blanket, 93

Homebody Blanket, 94–97

Yamhill Blanket, 98

Bobo Scarf, 19

brioche knitting

Lenny Scarf, 36

Morrison Cowl, 51

Radius Hooded Cowl, 55

technique, 112

Brooklyn Tweed, Quarry, 127

## C

Cada Día Beanie, 69

Cascades Cowl, 44

cast on, 113

Chelsea Arm Knit Cowl, 52

Clark Cowl, 48

colorful linen stitch

    Multnomah Beanie, 61

    technique, 114

Cotton Rope (Modern Macramé), 127

cowls, 41

    Cascades Cowl, 44

    Chelsea Arm Knit Cowl, 52

    Clark Cowl, 48

    La Tortuga Cowl, 47

    Morrison Cowl, 51

    Radius Hooded Cowl, 55–56

    Rhaye Cowl, 43

Crazy Sexy Wool (Wool and the Gang), 128

## D

dog items. *See* pet items

Don's Night Cap, 74

double moss stitch

    Nanay's Scarf, 39

    technique, 115

    Walter's Ottoman, 101

## E

Ember's Circle Rug, 89

Encore Mega Colorspun (Plymouth), 127

## F

Furniture: Walter's Ottoman, 101–102

## G

garter stitch

    Bobo Scarf, 19

    Clark Cowl, 48

    Homebody Blanket, 94

    La Tortuga Cowl, 47

    Lenny Scarf, 36

    Lombard Scarf, 28

    PNW Beanie, 65

    technique, 115

    Willamette Scarf, 24

## H

half brioche stitch

    Lenny Scarf, 36

    technique, 115

hats

    Cada Día Beanie, 69

    Don's Night Cap, 74

    Miss Van's Balaclava, 70–73

    Multnomah Beanie, 61–62

    PNW Beanie, 65–66

Hella Big Arm Knit Scarf, 32–35

herringbone stitch

    Miss Van's Balaclava, 70

    technique, 116–117

    Winston's Mat, 83

    Yamhill Blanket, 98

Homebody Blanket, 94–97

home pieces, 87

    Blacksheep's Arm Knit Blanket, 93

    Ember's Circle Rug, 89

    Homebody Blanket, 94

    Rhythm Rug, 90

    Walter's Ottoman, 101–102

    Yamhill Blanket, 98

horizontal invisible seam stitch

    Chelsea Arm Knit Cowl, 52

    Clark Cowl, 48

    Jax Scarf, 80

    Paco's Pillow, 84

    techniques, 117

Hygge (Woolfolk), 128

## I

I-cord

    technique, 118

    Tug-o-War Toy, 79

intarsia technique, 13

    Bobo Scarf, 19

    Rose City Scarf, 20

    technique, 119–120

    Tilikum Scarf, 15

    Willamette Scarf, 24

## J

Jax Scarf, 80

join in the round

    Cada Día Beanie, 69

    Cascades Cowl, 44

    Don's Night Cap, 74

    Ember's Circle Rug, 89

    La Tortuga Cowl, 47

    Morrison Cowl, 51

    Multnomah Beanie, 61

    Paco's Pillow, 84

    PNW Beanie, 65

    Radius Hooded Cowl, 55

    Rhaye Cowl, 43

    technique, 119

## L

La Tortuga Cowl, 47

Lenny Scarf, 36

Lombard Scarf, 28–31

loop stitch

    technique, 121–122

    Willamette Scarf, 24

Love Fest Fibers

    ReLove Alpaca, 128

    Tough Love, 127

## M

Miss Van's Balaclava, 70–73

mistake rib

    Cascades Cowl, 44

    technique, 121

Modern Macramé, Cotton Rope, 127

Morrison Cowl, 51

Multnomah Beanie, 61–62

## N

Nanay's Scarf, 39

## O

Ottoman, Walter's, 101–102

## P

Paco's Pillow, 84

pet items, 77

    Jax Scarf, 80

    Paco's Pillow, 84

    Tug-o-War Toy, 79

    Winston's Mat, 83

Pillow, Paco's, 84

Plymouth

    Encore Mega Colorspun, 127

    Viento, 128

PNW Beanie, 65–66

pompoms, 62

projects

    Blacksheep's Arm Knit Blanket, 93

    Bobo Scarf, 19

    Cada Día Beanie, 69

    Cascades Cowl, 44

    Chelsea Arm Knit Cowl, 52

    Clark Cowl, 48

    Don's Night Cap, 74

    Ember's Circle Rug, 89

    Hella Big Arm Knit Scarf, 32–35

    Homebody Blanket, 94–97

    Jax Scarf, 80

La Tortuga Cowl, 47

Lenny Scarf, 36

Lombard Scarf, 28–31

Miss Van's Balaclava, 70–73

Morrison Cowl, 51

Multnomah Beanie, 61–62

Nanay's Scarf, 39

Paco's Pillow, 84

PNW Beanie, 65–66

Radius Hooded Cowl, 55–56

Rhaye Cowl, 43

Rhythm Rug, 90

Rose City Scarf, 20–23

Tilikum Scarf, 15–16

Tug-o-War Toy, 79

Walter's Ottoman, 101–102

Willamette Scarf, 24–27

Winston's Mat, 83

Yamhill Blanket, 98

## Q

Quarry (Brooklyn Tweed), 127

## R

Radius Hooded Cowl, 55–56

ReLove Alpaca (Love Fest Fibers), 128

Rhaye Cowl, 43

Rhythm Rug, 90

Rose City Scarf, 20–23

rugs

    Ember's Circle Rug, 89

    Rhythm Rug, 90

## S

scarves, 13

    Bobo Scarf, 19

    Hella Big Arm Knit Scarf, 32–35

    Jax Scarf, 80

    Lenny Scarf, 36

    Lombard Scarf, 28–31

    Nanay's Scarf, 39

    Rose City Scarf, 20–23

    Tilikum Scarf, 15–16

    Willamette Scarf, 24–27

skull cap: Don's Night Cap, 74

slip stitch

    technique, 123

    Walter's Ottoman, 101

Squiggly (Woolly Mahoosive), 128

stitch abbreviations, 105–106

stitches

double moss stitch, 39, 101, 115

garter stitch, 19, 24, 28, 36, 47, 48, 65, 94, 115

half brioche stitch, 36, 115

herringbone stitch, 70, 83, 98, 115–117

horizontal invisible seam stitch, 48, 52, 80, 84, 117

loop stitch, 24, 121022

slip stitch, 101, 123

stockinette stitch, 52, 55, 80, 89, 90, 93, 123

stockinette stitch

Blacksheep's Arm Knit Blanket, 93

Chelsea Arm Knit Cowl, 52

Ember's Circle Rug, 89

Jax Scarf, 80

Radius Hooded Cowl, 55

Rhythm Rug, 90

technique, 123

## T

techniques

3-needle bind off, 55, 124–125

alternate rib cast on, 44, 69, 111

arm knitting, 32, 52, 93, 109–110

basketweave pattern, 43, 111

brioche, 36, 51, 55, 112

cast on, 113

colorful linen stitch, 61, 114

double moss stitch, 39, 101, 115

garter stitch, 19, 24, 28, 36, 47, 48, 65, 94, 115

half brioche stitch, 36, 115

herringbone stitch, 70, 83, 98, 116–117

horizontal invisible seam stitch, 48, 52, 80, 84, 117

I-cord, 79, 118

intarsia, 13, 15, 19, 20, 24, 119–120

join in the round, 43, 44, 47, 51, 55, 61, 65, 69, 74, 84, 89, 119

loop stitch, 24, 121–122

mistake rib, 44, 121

slip stitch, 101, 123

stockinette stitch, 52, 55, 80, 89, 90, 93, 123

twisted rib, 61, 69, 70, 74, 80, 124

3-needle bind off

Radius Hooded Cowl, 55

technique, 124–125

Tilikum Scarf, 15–16

Tough Love (Love Fest Fibers), 127

Tug-o-War Toy, 79

twisted rib

Cada Día Beanie, 69

Don's Night Cap, 74

Jax Scarf, 80

Miss Van's Balaclava, 70

Multnomah Beanie, 61

technique, 124

## V

Viento (Plymouth), 128

## W

Walter's Ottoman, 101–102

Willamette Scarf, 24–27

Winston's Mat, 83

Wool and the Gang, Crazy Sexy Wool, 128

Woolfolk, Hygge, 128

Woolly Mahoosive, Squiggly, 128

## Y

Yamhill Blanket, 98

yarn, 127–128